WHATEVER
HAPPENED
TO QUEER
HAPPINESS?
KEVIN
BRAZIL

Published by Influx Press
The Greenhouse, 49 Green Lanes, London, N16 9BU
www.influxpress.com
All Rights Reserved.
© Kevin Brazil 2022

First edition 2022. Printed and bound in the UK by TJ Books.

PAPERBACK ISBN: 9781910312957
EBOOK ISBN: 9781910312964

EDITOR: Kit Caless
COVER DESIGN: Keenan Designs
INTERIOR DESIGN: Vince Haig
COPY EDITOR: Natasha Onwuemezi

                                        happiness
the least and best of human attainments

(Frank O'Hara, 'Poem Read at Joan Mitchell's')

CONTENTS

Foreword: On Crowds   7

What Ever Happened to Queer Happiness?   11
The Lives of Samuel Steward   39
The Queer Uses of Art   67
Fear of a Gay Planet   89
Dungeness   115
Félix and Cathy   143
Looking Like Wolfgang   169
Dancing On Our Own   195

Works Discussed   225
Acknowledgements   231

FOREWORD: ON CROWDS

I've always felt at home in a crowd. I haven't lived long enough to be able to say that this is the only time I've ever felt truly at home, but crowds have been something I've returned to over and over again, and what we return to is, for me, is one definition of home. Home as something we do, not somewhere we go. For the crowd offers a home that isn't a specific place, but rather one which is made up of the relationships we form with others, never perfectly known, as they drift in and out of our awareness.

Every time I exit Liverpool Street Station after a journey back to London, something inside me unlocks. To the infinite inhabitants of the city, I am no one, which means there is always the potential I can become anyone. In an art gallery or a library, I am among people united, if only for an hour and in silence, by the things we are drawn to, not what we appear to be. Our loves, our obsessions, our confusingly ambivalent attachments. And in the intimate darkness of a dancefloor, in the basement of a club or underneath a morning sky, I've never felt more like the body I am.

These are crowds in which we hover between anonymity and acknowledgement. We are neither so alienated from one another that we feel we owe nothing to those we encounter, and so consume them as spectacles, nor can we indulge in the fantasy that others can ever be so known to us to be purely transparent, or that who they are can be summed up under a label or a name. Crowds are assemblages in which we can experience ourselves not as individuals, but as the kinds of relationships we have with other people. People whose presence can be sensed, not scrolled away; whose presence can be withdrawn, not surveilled against their will.

Crowds create opportunities for risk and exploration, for touches that can be refused as much as welcomed. Their boundaries remain in flux as people enter and exit of their own accord. Crowds, however, are no utopia, for to imagine the crowd as a utopia – the place that is no place – would be to lift it out of its embedding in time and space, history and geography. Every crowd is formed on an unequal terrain, irrespective of whether those inequalities are visible or not, and forms one itself in turn. I make my way through a crowd with all the power acting through my particular body – white, cisgender, and able – and all the hesitancy constraining my particular desires, desires I need to enter the crowd to discover. Yet, this too, for me, has always been one promise of the crowd. To bring differences to awareness for those who want to see them. When you find you are suddenly lost in a crowd, in a position that you have never been before, you can experience yourself not as what you always have been, but what you might become in a different relationship with others.

These essays were written over a number of years, in times of isolation, both personal and collective. They assemble a crowd, living and dead, through which I have explored my relationship to the idea of queer happiness. How to tell stories of happiness, in all their complexity, so they can be remembered. How I have tried and failed to find that happiness in my own life. How these stories need to be preserved, not to keep things the same, but to enable new desires, new lives, and new crowds to come into being. That exploration, and the figures it gathers, is marked by the particularity of who I am, what I desire, and what writing enables anyone to be. It offers nothing like a definition; its figures constitute nothing like a canon. These essays simply offer a record of my attachments to some members of a larger crowd; a crowd others can choose to join, transform, or leave, as they seek out those who might, one day, make them happy.

WHAT EVER HAPPENED TO QUEER HAPPINESS?

'I feel that every good thing that has happened in my life has come from being queer.'

Sometimes a line just won't let go. Sometimes a line just sticks.

It was the conclusion to an interview with Andrea Lawlor about their novel, *Paul Takes the Form of a Mortal Girl* (2017). It seemed carefully chosen, as if to pose a parting challenge: is this true for you? Logically, it couldn't be. I have two parents and three siblings, who are mundanely, gloriously, and definitionally straight. Some of my best friends are straight. Many of my favourite writers and most of my favourite artists. But logic has little to do with it. That line stuck to me because I stuck to it.

What had left me so sticky, like cool sweat on a warm thigh? Maybe I was failing as a reader, a listener, a looker. Or maybe I was the only one thinking that for about a decade or so, at least in those places that proclaim themselves to be the mainstream of literary culture and, in the work of a new generation of writers, queerness seemed only allowed to enter that space so long as it was confessed as being the source of every bad thing in one's life: trauma, abuse, rejection, destructive relationships, damaged selves. The full spectrum of extraordinary unhappiness.

A friend once said of top surgery that no matter how much you look forward to it, it's only when it happens that you realise exactly what had been missing. You never can wholly control the things you cling to. But you can figure out what has made you the sticky surface you are.

* * *

'From my childhood, I have no happy memories.' The first line of Édouard Louis' *The End of Eddy* (2014), a novel that achieved international acclaim in the years that saw the rise of the far-right in France, for its dissection of the relationship between xenophobia and homophobia among the country's white working class. It announces from the start the absence of happiness from its world. That world, as well as featuring appalling poverty and violence, is where the narrator becomes aware of his desire and the social meaning of that desire. The first time he hears it named – *You're the faggot, right?* – he is spat on by two other children, and the name and the spit are 'inscribed onto me permanently like stigmata'.

For Louis, to be baptised by the spit of others is to be sanctified by an incurable wound, a baptism so unlike that imagined by his predecessor Jean Genet. In *Our Lady of the*

Flowers (1943), the gobs of spit that fall upon the body of the narrator, intended to shame him into silence, bloom into a garland of roses. Louis' suffering leaves him unable, or unwilling, to understand the pain of others. 'I don't know how she felt when she said things like that to me,' he responds when his mother describes accidentally losing a pregnancy into a toilet bowl. The most he can do, with the benefit of an elite education, is to believe that 'many modes of discourse intersected in my mother and spoke through her'. Unlike the narrator, she is not an individual with a history but a category of sociological theory. The violence he suffers destroys his ability to see others as individuals, and yet it provides the material for a memoir disguised as a novel, a book that becomes his claim to individuality and enables him to change his name from the faggot Eddy Bellegueule to the writer Édouard Louis.

That to be gay is to be defined by suffering is the premise of the baroque symphony of trauma that is Hanya Yanagihara's *A Little Life* (2015), as much as the solo recital of shame that is Garth Greenwell's *What Belongs to You* (2016). To be gay is to suffer among Puerto Rican New York in Justin Torres's *We the Animals* (2011), among the Vietnamese Americans of Ocean Vuong's *On Earth We're Briefly Gorgeous* (2019), among affluent Nigerians in Uzodinma Iweala's *Speak No Evil* (2018) and in Communist Poland in Tomasz Jedrowski's *Swimming in the Dark* (2020).

Yet, there can be unintended consequences to defining yourself by your suffering. What makes Louis' second novel, *A History of Violence* (2016), so compelling is his dawning awareness of the solipsism his suffering imposes upon him. This novel reveals the conflict between the narrator's demand that his pain is accounted for and his commitment to solidarity, one that extends to trying to refuse to prosecute a Kabyle man who rapes him due to the racism of the French police system. The events leading to the rape are recounted by Édouard himself, and by his sister Clara, who tells Édouard's account to her husband while Édouard secretly listens.

Clara also digresses to give her version of what happened when Édouard came out to his family, while Édouard, author and narrator, interjects. 'We told him all that mattered was his happiness, all we cared about was he was happy (*she's lying*) . . . we accepted him as he was (*not true*)'. But then the interruptions cease: 'Sometimes I think Édouard told us he was different not so we could be closer to him or know him better . . . but actually for the opposite reason. In his heart, he didn't want us to accept him.' 'What I think', she continues, 'is that once he saw we accepted him, secrets and all, it made him hate us. He hated us because it ruined his plans, he couldn't go and tell everyone how everything was our fault, and sometimes I think he never forgave us for accepting him how he is. That's if you ask me.' Clara draws our attention to the limits imposed by founding one's identity on suffering. When identity is bought at the cost of solidarity with others, that individuality is forever mortgaged to unhappiness.

In contrast, Didier, an older friend of Édouard, modelled on the sociologist Didier Eribon, believes that 'the things we remember most clearly', that make us who we are, 'are always those that bring us shame'. And it is with a reminder of this interlacing of unhappiness, writing and individuality that the book ends, by quoting from Imre Kertész's *Kaddish for an Unborn Child* (1990): 'It turned out that it is impossible to write about happiness, or at least I can't, which in this case amounts to the same thing after all; happiness is perhaps too simple to let itself be written about . . . a life lived in happiness is therefore a life lived in muteness'. Writing a story of unhappiness, at least for Louis, is the way to create oneself in writing. But what happens if stories of queer happiness can never be written and the lives that lived them are forever forgotten?

* * *

It's not just gay men; it's not just novels. In Alison Bechdel's *Fun Home* (2006), a graphic memoir so influential its author's name gave us the Bechdel test – does a work feature two women in a scene without a man where they don't talk about a man? – unhappiness about queer sexuality gives the imagery its very colour and form. Bechdel's father, whose repressed affairs with young men were hidden from his children until after a suspected suicide, transmutes his shame and self-loathing into renovating the family home with 'meticulous period interiors', work mirrored by Bechdel's own intricate drawings of him and the Gothic wooden house panels she painted in muted monochrome. That palette, light grey on dark, is used to highlight, in a panel depicting the full and various dictionary entry, *Fun Home's* definitions of queerness: 'At variance with what is usual or normal in character, appearance, or action… strange… suspicious … qualmish; faint… to thwart, ruin; to put (one) in a bad position… Counterfeit.' Queerness isolates each member of the family; another panel shows the house in cross-section, with each family member ensconced in a circle, absorbed in their separate pursuits: writing, drawing, creating. Queerness produces isolation, isolation produces creativity, creativity produces Bechdel's ability to draw, and that produces *Fun Home*. And *In the Dream House* (2019) by Carmen Maria Machado, *Difficult Women* (2017) by Roxane Gay, *The Lonely City* (2016) by Olivia Laing . . .

Lists aren't evidence; lists aren't arguments; listing is barely even thinking. But sometimes, lists can help us see what our faith in thinking can't.

* * *

Limp wrists,
Cocked hips,
Buzz cuts,
Dungarees,
Biker boots,
Armband tattoos,
Scars on show at the pool.

* * *

Maybe it was ever thus, *Fun Home* suggests. Maybe queer writing was always born from isolation. For Bechdel, realising that she was a lesbian was at first 'a revelation not of the flesh, but of the mind'. She trawls through the library, and one panel shows her hand grasping *The Well of Loneliness* (1928) by Radclyffe Hall, another a stack of books including E.M. Forster's *Maurice*, first completed in 1914. Stories in which to be openly lesbian, unlike the grammatical disguises of Gertrude Stein, is to be condemned to loneliness; stories in which to be happily gay, unlike the evasions of Marcel Proust, is to be unpublishable until 1971.

Bechdel's copy of *Maurice* is stacked in a pile with the books complied by those who rebelled against this litany of shame: *Out of the Closets and Into the Streets* and *Our Bodies, Ourselves*: anthologies of the liberation movements of the 1960s and 1970s, anthologies under the banner of rebellion: PRIDE. For many, Pride parades are about coming together to show the world you are proud, to show that being gay can mean exactly what it seems – that you are happy! But pride only adds a glittering surface to the currents of shame that have flowed through queer writing, art, and cinema since the 1960s, 'as if pride were not the first manifestation of shame', as Louis reminds us in *The End of Eddy*.

Academic queer theory sometimes appears to take pride in the shame it studies. This is in part a reaction to the more simplistically affirmative kinds of gay, lesbian and trans histories that were produced after the 1970s. Books like Bechdel's *Out of the Closets and Into the Streets*, books that showed we were always here, we haven't always suffered, we too can be happy. But the odd effect of universities defining themselves as the space that resists more optimistic attitudes to being queer is that the more negative approaches become aligned with those who are more 'educated', who have had their positivity dispelled by taking 'Introduction to Queer Theory'. To be educated into queerness is also to be educated into shame, or a more sophisticated understanding of shame.

The queer theorist Heather Love tells the story of an academic conference on gay shame held in the United States in 2003, in which the organisers invited political activists from the Gay Shame movement, which had been set up in the 1990s in New York and San Francisco to fight gentrification and the commodification of queer culture. To the activists, the academics were fetishising gay shame as an object of study rather than mobilising for change. To the academics, the activists were instrumental in a different way – they were only interested in shame as an impulse for action, unwilling, or unable, to spend time investigating the complex effects of mobilising shame in a political struggle. No matter who was right, this was a battle over who gets to own shame, who gets to claim to be the most unhappy. It was as if this were the greatest prize a queer could obtain.

Asking why queerness has been so persistently associated with unhappiness can devolve into asking: well, that depends on how you define queerness in the first place, doesn't it? These literary canons and academic conferences are signposts to the swamp that is finding a universally agreed definition of queerness. Definitions matter, not because they can be true, but because of what they enable you to do. Point, demarcate, draw boundaries in order to take up space. Definitions also shouldn't matter for the same reasons. What is important is what they end up doing, irrespective of what we believe they mean.

This means not asking why queerness seems defined by unhappiness but looking at what queerness is doing in writing and at what kinds of writing are doing queerness. Not what is queerness, but how it is being written?

* * *

One night I went out to a garage in South London to a night run by and for women, womxn and those who reject such categories as tools of oppression. I was made to wait longer than my friends at the door, my fate decided by three butches in leather jackets and biker boots with magnetic, confident smiles. Inside, the music was hard, fast, and dark, and I soon lost my friends, who had other things on their minds. I found myself the only visible man among a group of strangers, and gradually, without noticing it at first, we all began to move in loose unison: legs whipping out and bodies jacking back, over and over again. No one paid any attention to me; I played no part in the currents of desire that were swirling all around me, but my body, and its difference, for how long, I can't remember, were invited to belong.

One night, I went with a friend to a warehouse in Manchester to dance all Sunday. On the train there, we cried; on the train back, we saw Wolfgang Tillmans. Sometime in the afternoon, my friend took me into a room where the only person who wasn't a bearded gay man was a girl leaning against the wall, wearing a necklace that said TECHNOFEMINISM, who barely danced but just smiled. Soon, a woman's voice was singing a chorus over and over again, and everyone joined in, and it was played on loop for so long that I learned the words and joined in, singing with hundreds of the hardest-looking men, preening and weeping as if centre on the stages of a hundred little operas. I didn't need to know the song to become just another diva in the crowd performing for an audience of one.

One night, I went out clubbing with my then-boyfriend and queued for an hour so he could be at the front of the dancefloor with his people, young Black kids there to see a Black trans woman sell out a club. Those tickets were also sold, it turned out, to a group of tiny Italian lesbians as well as to bankers in shirts and jackets. No one needed to say a thing; no one could say anything over the mixing of gospel choirs and deep bass as the bankers began to crush the lesbians up against the DJ booth. That boyfriend and I spread ourselves into a shield to give those women the space they needed to dance alone and the pleasure of dancing alone, yet together.

* * *

I knew that I was what the world named gay as early as I can remember, but I'd never heard the word queer as anything other than an insult until I arrived at university. That might be a reason why endless arguments about what it means to be queer have felt to me to be unavoidable yet somehow dispensable. I know I live the life it is trying to name, but I know that life can be lived without that name. And I've never felt that life more intensely than in those moments in warehouses and clubs when people with different desires, desires that need to exclude others to be fulfilled, nevertheless come together to make something collective. Nothing so grand as a culture, nothing so bound to time as a generation, nothing so fixed as an identity, but some kind of collaborative loosening of the constraints of individuality produced by the collective difference of our desires.

The American scholar Saidiya Hartman, who has devoted her life to studying the legacy of slavery in Black American life, was once asked in an interview: 'How do you define joy – what does joy mean to you?' She replied:

'I tend to describe joy as this experience of transformation or release from the constraint or costume of the individual or the subject into this other form. So, for me, I think it's about floating, it's about being nothing and being everything at the same time; this sense of the self-disappearing in the context of the vastness of the earth, the ocean, the sky, the land. That kind of joy is always about self-dissolution, escape.'

Is this what it means to be happy? In those clubs, the presence of other people's desires and embodiments produced those moments where I felt suspended in that strange place between individuality and the collective, neither one nor the other, neither different nor the same, certain these were not my experiences alone, certain I was not writing the story that is 'me'.

* * *

The Chateau
Cocktail d'Amore
Aphrodyki
Fire
Pantibar
Lab.oratory
Big Dyke Energy

* * *

Is there any way of writing about happiness, queer or otherwise, that isn't obnoxious? Or boring? Is there any way of speaking about happiness that isn't a form of saying: 'I've survived; why couldn't you?' Is there any way of talking about happiness that doesn't also ask: 'Shouldn't you be trying harder?'

Maybe it isn't possible to write about happiness at all. *'Le bonheur écrit à l'encre blanche sur des pages blanches,'* wrote Henri de Montherlant. 'Happiness writes in white ink on a white page.' Happiness leaves no trace on a state of blankness, and it is happiness because it leaves no trace. In moments of happiness, we are not recording, we are not transcribing, we are not remembering. We have not yet split ourselves between past and future, the split that takes place with every act of writing. These pencil marks, these dark pixels: messages to the future versions of ourselves who will no longer be what they are now. Who will no longer be happy.

Or is it just that happiness writes in a colour we don't know how to read? Secret lovers also write in white, and spies and undercover agents entrust what is most important to lemon juice and invisible ink. The safest way to send a message on your phone is to ensure it deletes itself once it is read. Anarchist programmers have devoted a labour of love to make your encrypted message disappear into a luminous white screen.

For Freud, happiness appeared to be the purpose of life implicit in all human actions: human beings 'strive for happiness, they want to become happy and remain so'. Yet for Freud, 'what we call happiness, in the strictest sense of the word, arises from the fairly sudden satisfaction of pent-up needs', merely a physiological state of pleasure. It was, therefore, a product of the pleasure principle, and this 'is quite incapable of being realized; all the institutions of the universe are opposed to it; one is inclined to say that the intention that man should be "happy" has no part in the plan of "creation"'. The act of sexual love, he continued, 'had afforded man the most potent experiences of satisfaction and had actually supplied him with the model for all happiness' with the consequence that he would 'go on seeking his happiness in the sphere of sexual relations and place genital eroticism at the centre of his life'. But, for Freud, this was a mistake. The belief that the state produced by sex is happiness is an illusion that the pleasure principle sets up to mask the true insatiability of desire. In fact, that we believe sex can make us happy is the very source of our unhappiness. This is the lesson the psychoanalyst teaches. They enlighten us to the unavoidable sadness our sexuality will cause us and help us to cope (for an hourly fee). One might be inclined to say that for Freud, happiness has no part in the plan of sexuality.

The process by which one learns this lesson, either in therapy or elsewhere, furnishes a person with their unique response to this universal structure of sadness: desire is caused by a lack that can never be satisfied. This may be the human condition, but how we come to learn this lesson gives us the story of our individual lives. This is one reason why psychoanalysis, or therapy in general, can be seen as an extended exercise in writing a kind of autobiography. While sexual 'happiness' may be an illusion, to discover how you cope with this condition is to discover who you are. Freud hardly invented the belief that suffering individualises. It is a belief as central to Christianity, with its demands for secret confessions, as it is to Buddhism and its conviction that to escape suffering requires escaping the self. Yet Freud's theory of sexuality, and all that's descended from it, has left us with the belief that while sex is something that can never make us truly or fully happy, the story of how we live with our unhappiness is the story of our individual lives. It is the story that makes us an individual.

* * *

Fairuz
Meena
Umm Kulthum
Nina
Mariah
Charli
Whitney
Cher

* * *

Given the following, produce the equation that solves for (x): Why is queer happiness so difficult to write about?

One: Tolstoy. 'All happy families are alike; each unhappy family is unhappy in its own way'; or, all happy stories are the same.

Two: Freud. The story of how we suffer sexuality is the story of who we are; or, unhappiness makes us individuals.

Divide by the common factor: happiness is the absence of a sense of individuality.

A solution: happiness cannot be written about in a first-person autobiographical form?

Both the premise and the solution to this equation may be nothing but mere speculation, and speculation might not be the most immediately useful mode of thinking about queer happiness. (Although, when Freud invented the pleasure principle, he admitted that: 'What follows is speculation, often farfetched speculation' – and look how far that got him.)

What these equations provide is one theory for why so much recent queer writing seems to be so preoccupied with its unhappiness. The reason lies less in their queer content but in their autobiographical form. Or rather, a form that we might want to call 'autobiography-adjacent', rather than 'autofiction' – a term that tries to do too much in naming a genre rather than a tendency, and that names nothing distinctive about contemporary writing. There is nothing in terms of literary form that the Chris Krauses of the world are doing that wasn't done as early as the 1960s by those nadirs of male heterosexuality John Updike, Philip Roth and Norman 'fugging' Mailer.

Call them what you want; works of fiction that model themselves on autobiography, confession, or memoir have hardly been the exclusive product of queer writers. Yet queer writing, like that produced by any group made into a minority, has its own reasons for tending towards the autobiographically adjacent. Faggot, dyke, poof, pervert. I'll tell you what your gender is, I'll tell you who you can marry, I'll decide whether you are under threat of persecution. Oppression may be structural, but it works by taking away your individuality. Reclaiming that individuality by showing, in writing, that you have a story of your own becomes a means of resistance.

Oppression ties another knot in the braiding of autobiography and unhappiness. It oppresses by denying your individuality and denying the existence of the pain this denial causes. You fight back by asserting your individuality and everything you have suffered in one and the same act of writing. Yet the rules according to which you must fight back are rigged, and everyone knows this. People who transition

know they have to tell a story of traumatic dysphoria to
get the care they should be owed by right alone. Gays and
lesbians know they have to tell a story of how not being able
to get married is an unbearable injustice, not because they
dream of the state blessing their monogamy, but because
they just want the option, same as anyone else. Stories that
individualise by detailing unhappiness have the power of a
certain kind of resistance, but it's a resistance built into the
structure of domination itself. That's why, after a while, all the
stories of queer suffering strangely start to sound the same,
as if beneath a thousand melodic variations, you realise they
have all been written in the same key. These stories are not
nearly as individualising as they claim to be because they all
purchase their individuality by the scale of their suffering.

Autobiography isn't wedded to unhappiness, but it
has been having affairs with misery ever since Augustine's
Confessions. This book was as consequential for autobiography
as a form as it was for Christianity as a religion in the way it
blamed so much of the shame Augustine experienced on 'the
lust of the flesh . . . ruinous to those whom it enslaves'. His
Confessions gain their sense of drama because, like all good
stories, they are the story of a struggle: 'Even if human beings
delight in the law of God in their inmost selves, what will
they do about the other law in their members which is at war
with the law of their minds?' Augustine was a theological
influence on the Reformation, but his *Confessions* were also
a literary model for those Protestants who, liberated from
the institutional control of the Catholic Church, submitted
themselves instead to injunctions of their conscience to
confess every lustful and concupiscent thought in diaries,
pamphlets, and in front of congregations, with no small hint

of hypocritical erotic thrill. Jean-Jacques Rousseau initiated modern autobiography in many ways, not least by sparing us no detail of his struggle with 'that vice which shame and timidity find so convenient': masturbation. One of the strangest reversals in literary history is that confessional and autobiographical writing have come to be seen as effeminate, soft, unintellectual – written by those who are just *too much*. It wasn't the feminine who told us, in detail, about the movements of their uncontrollable members; it wasn't the femmes who needed us to know about their habit, when they desired someone, of jacking off into their empty beds.

Of course, there can be memoirs and autobiographies of happiness, queer or otherwise. The title of Jeanette Winterson's *Why Be Happy When You Could Be Normal* (2011), her memoir of a childhood spent growing up in the working-class North, was the response of her evangelical Christian adoptive mother to Winterson coming out as a lesbian. Yet even her attempt to claim queer happiness involves a disavowal. 'Pursuing happiness,' she writes, 'is not at all the same as being happy – which I think is fleeting, dependent upon circumstances, and a bit bovine.' Who could be so stupid as to want to be happy? She rather seeks the *happ* in the Old English root of happiness, 'the fate, the draw that is yours'. The fate of queer writing that touches on autobiography has been forced, by reasons of the form and the world in which it is written, into the confession of unhappiness. Its fate has been like those childhood experiments designed to show phototropism in plants, where seeds are planted in a cardboard box with a hole cut in one side. Just as seedlings tend towards the only source of light they sense, their bodies growing warped yet beautiful in their own way, so too queer autobiography bends towards the source of the only visibility on offer.

Queer writers know the boxes they live in; queer writers of colour know it twice over. An early poem in Danez Smith's first collection *[insert] boy* (2014) offers the disclaimer 'I am sorry I have no happy poems' to make us ask: why is that? In their later collection, *Homie* (2020), 'confession old & new' wryly reflects on what it means to write about their HIV diagnosis: 'that which hasn't killed you yet can pay the rent / if you play it right.' In *Against Memoir* (2018), Michelle Tea admits that for her, writing memoir is 'a compulsion on par with alcoholism'. It is an addiction to returning to experiences of trauma in order to master them, and it is an addiction to 'the story line,' a narrative about the self that perpetuates the very idea of the self even when 'as Buddhism insists, there is no "self"'. Autobiographical writing is a way to cope with suffering by creating, in writing, a self that has survived. But that self is created only insofar as it has suffered. Tea doesn't want to get clean from confessional writing and the self it gives her, but she does wonder: 'What would it mean to get sober from memoir?'

* * *

Checking in,
Holding Space
Boundaries
Care
Capacity
Breathing
Perception is Projection.

* * *

It is striking what happens to friendship in these stories of queer unhappiness; that is, if friends ever appear at all. Friends are understandably absent from Louis' childhood, yet even though they sustain him through his rape, they fleetingly appear only as sources of sexual comfort or conduits of the social capital accorded by his new life in Paris. Bechdel's *Fun Home* could provide another test bearing her name: is there a scene where two queer friends appear without, and without discussing, their family trauma or their fucked-up lovers? The title of Sally Rooney's *Conversation with Friends* (2017) might suggest its heart is a friendship between two queer women, Frances and Bobbi, but the conversations Bobbi offers only serve to build Frances a self that can go back to her male lover at the end of the novel. The great exception is Yanagihara's *A Little Life*, where the friendship between four men is a constant across hundreds of pages of pain. Yet these friendships are unable to prevent one character, Jude, from succumbing to suicide caused by a childhood of sexual abuse. Friendship is nothing, as artistic material or a source of care, when faced with the dark power of sexual trauma.

This is strange in the broader history of queer life since that life has long involved the cultivation of friendships as a collective source of happiness that either replaces a homophobic family or, in more benign versions, compliments the reproductive family by offering something it can't. That friendships can be a 'chosen family' is a gift from queer life to the world that has seeped into mainstream culture through shows like *Pose*. But calling these friendships a 'chosen family' or 'alternative kinship structure' betrays a sad failure of nerve. As if the greatest honour that could be bestowed upon friendships is that they could be like the family they are not; as if the deepest source of care will only ever come from a 'Mother'. The queer theorist Sam McBean instead likens these bonds of friendships to a 'network'. You care and are cared for, sustain and are sustained, not within the imaginative horizons of Mommy, Daddy and Me, but within a web that includes you and yet extends beyond you. Sustaining these bonds takes work, and this work returns to you in time, but not always as the balancing of debit and credit that takes place between two people. You might not get what you need from the person to which you give, but it will come back from another who is given and getting from others in turn.

The image of friendship as a network might also suggest the kind of happiness that friendship can provide, in contrast to the satisfaction and lack of desire. The pleasure we get from sex has often been described as a loss of the sense of individuality, what Freud called an 'oceanic feeling'. Our boundaries dissolve, we lose ourselves in another, we return to the undifferentiated belonging we experienced in the womb. A network, however – whether we picture that as computers linking up to create the internet or as the fish, corals and luminous algae that make up an underwater reef – is, by definition, made up of more than two. Its members neither dissolve into the ocean nor remain isolated individuals in their shells. They are suspended between being a part and a whole, between being an individual and collective. As in Hartman's description of joy, we are released from 'the costume of the individual or the subject', not into the formless anonymity of the sea, but 'into this other form'. The web, the network, the reef; it's where I've always found my shelter.

* * *

Arthur
Tom
Bella
Luke
Oonagh
Sarah
Zara
Sam

* * *

Memoir might be an addiction for the way in which it helps us cope with suffering. Such, at least, is the most charitable interpretation. But to slide from this to the claim that people are unhappy because they are addicted to their suffering is to be lubricated by the cruellest kind of self-help optimism. Unhappy? The problem is you. Getting sober from memoir is not getting sober from sadness, depression, or pain. It is about stepping away from a certain kind of writing: first-person, retrospective, luxuriating in the display of its wounds. This writing might create a self that has survived, but it might not create a self that has known happiness. Happiness, or queer happiness at least, may be a matter of the form of the stories we tell about ourselves. We may need to change the form of these stories to find a way to remember those chance moments of blankness, dissolution or merging into others that happiness might inescapably be. And changing the form of these stories might enable us to step away from a certain idea of who we are: individual, unique, the source of the only story that matters.

The only person you should listen to about getting sober is someone who has been an addict. The only people you should trust to tell you about happiness are those who have known its opposites.

Lou Sullivan was born in 1951 and kept a diary from the age of ten until his death, aged thirty-nine, in 1991. He was born into a world that designated him a girl who would grow up to be a woman. Over the course of his life, Lou became one of the first publicly known people to transition to being a man, according to the medicalised model of gender transition, one where people have to admit to suffering the 'illness' of gender dysphoria in order to receive treatment and be 'cured', and, back then, a model in which men who wanted that treatment had to confess an attraction to women and only women. Through a life of activism, Sullivan and others changed this model to one where some (but not enough) people can get the medical care they need to live in their bodies and realise their desire by right, just like any other kind of medical care. For these reasons, Sullivan has long been a sort of father figure to trans men in general and gay trans men in particular, someone whose story belongs, importantly but not exclusively, to a specific group of people.

Alongside a teenage obsession with the Beatles and leather boots, an early desire appears in his diaries: 'I want to be a beautiful man making love to a beautiful man.' The diaries track the changes in Sullivan's sense of self and the body in which he sensed them. But although Sullivan is an exquisite writer about sex, these diaries offer more than a detailed account of a changing anatomy. They present us with a view of what it means to be trans, gay and both at the same time. Sullivan knows that gender is not only an identity but also the expression of the desire of another; he feels most like a boy when his lover, J., 'thinks I am really a boy'. Sullivan knows the nature of this and all desire: 'I'm only carried off as long as whoever it is feeds the fantasy – if they act blatantly contrary to the image, it's shattered, and so is my passion, infatuation.' Sullivan experienced his desires being destroyed. Doctors rejected his first request for hormones because he presented himself not as a straight man but as a 'fruity little faggot'. He never completed his surgical transition because surgeons refused to carry out his final procedures after he contracted HIV.

He also believed 'I *am* going to live my life alone' and that 'if I am the only one I have, I have a right to make myself happy'. Even at the end of his life, believing he would 'forever be lacking' due to his incomplete surgery, Sullivan believed it had 'been worth all these years just to be in this bar, here, now, with AIDS and to be a man among men'. He still believed what he wrote as a teenager: 'I wanna look like what I am but don't know what someone like me looks like.' He wanted people to see a gay man, a trans man, but he wanted them to also see him as something else: 'I mean, when people look at me, I want them to think – there's one of those people that reasons, that is a philosopher, that has their own interpretation of happiness. That's what I am.'

The diaries tell us so much about what Sullivan wanted, but at least from within their pages, we can never know what he wanted for these diaries. They were clearly kept by someone who needed to write themselves into existence and, especially in later years, they were evidently kept by someone who believed a record of his life would be a help to others – just like Sullivan found succour in writing the biography of someone who transitioned before him, Jack Bee Garland. It is hard to know whether these diaries were meant to be material for an autobiography of his own or whether they were the only record he wanted to keep. Yet, for everything that these diaries capture and record, they nevertheless leave the reader with a lingering sense that their first-person form doesn't fully express the interpretation of happiness that Sullivan wants his life to be. Indeed, it is only because the diaries capture so much that they fully pursue the project of writing oneself in the first person that Sullivan can realise that his happiness can never be personal, individual, produced by himself alone.

The horizon of each diary entry is short: today's feelings, last night's fuck. It may be a consequence of this brevity, or the selection edited for publication or Sullivan's personality, but his diaries leave an impression that recording fleeting moments produces a model of the self that is hard to capture in other forms of writing. Sullivan captures with luminous clarity the way our sense of self is both ever-changing and produced out of interactions with others. One entry recounts that 'it's been happening more and more often that I am walking down the street and am looking appreciatively at a man, I see a sparkle in his eyes, and we smile and nod, acknowledging each other's appreciation. And when he's gone, I soar, I feel totally worthwhile, so satisfied with myself . . . that the isolation caused by my incomplete body is not all that important'. When writing in that bar, near the end of his life, what makes him feel like the self he has made has been worth it is that this is a self among others. Other gay men make him the man he wants to be: 'a man among men.' Recognition is achieved not by some endless struggle with the other, or a titanic Oedipal rivalry, but in the fleeting glance one gay man gives another as they pass on the street. If other gay men in this sense enable Sullivan to be happy with his body, his body enables others to understand what it means to be gay. For Sullivan, what he desires about 'male / male love' is 'The fact that it didn't just *happen* – that the two people involved really *wanted* to be with each other'. Queer happiness doesn't lie in the predetermined fate of *happ* that for Winterson is the etymological root of happiness and happenstance. It is wanting what isn't at first natural, or evident, or the way things initially seem, but the ability to see beyond what just happens is something only someone else can give you.

Queer happiness doesn't just happen. It isn't the produce of fate, the submission to a nature we imagine we can't change. Neither is it something anyone can create alone, a state we can achieve by tunnelling into our past. It can only happen if you expose yourself to others; not the exposure that comes from revealing your unique inner depths, but the exposure made possible by making yourself a moving body on a dancefloor or an open eye on the street, the random encounters that are the other meaning of the *happ* in happiness: fortune, luck, chance events and occurrences. These can only happen if you spread yourself into a network of connections, rather than spreading yourself open to reveal what is yours and yours alone. It can happen if you make yourself into a surface without ever knowing what will end up sticking to it.

Exposed surfaces are liable to wound; they are not the kind of glossy carapace that covers up what lies underneath. If writing about queer happiness involves anything, it does not require a disavowal of suffering or pain. But it might involve a disavowal of certain forms of writing about that pain. If queer writing has recently been dominated by stories of suffering, this is not because there is anything inherently unhappy about being queer, but because these stories have been largely taken the form of individual memoirs or autobiography-adjacent first-person fictions. Telling these individual stories will always be a means of resisting an oppression that takes away your individuality, that reduces you to a slur, a category, a collective object of shame. And they can be a means of coping with suffering by creating a self that has survived. But there are limits imposed by founding your identity on stories of individual suffering. That individuality is forever bound to unhappiness, and it is purchased at the cost of telling stories about your relations with others: other people, other places, other things. If queer happiness lies in those relations, or rather, in a certain kind of exposure to the possibility of those relations, then its writing will have to find a form to match that exposure. A form of connections and relations that gives shape to the work of connecting and relating; a form that is the good kind of clingy, lingering on that which sticks us to things; a form in which the self is created by its openness to others.

* * *

I was introduced to Sullivan's diaries by a friend of a friend called Jack, someone who joined a reading group to which

I also belonged. Each time our group met, we would read a book suggested by someone else – a book about queerness, sexuality, or gender, or just a book whose style we liked. At the end of one meeting, it was Jack's turn to suggest a book, and he proposed we read *The Diaries of Lou Sullivan*, which Jack had long known about, but which had just been published in an edited version. He wanted us to read Sullivan's diary because it was an important work of writing in itself and because Jack and Lou had more in common than both being gay trans men. As a child, Jack also kept a diary, in which, like Lou, he recalled recording the desire that when he grew up, he wanted to become a gay man. That being a gay man was something you could grow up wanting to be, not a burden you grew up negotiating when to reveal; that it could be something to be desired, not merely accepted; that what you are could be wanted, not just something that just happened: here was a way of seeing myself that I could only get from another, something that came from another being able to realise their desires, a lesson that I should create a world in which that realisation can happen. But this is something I could see if only I learned how to look. It was a happiness I never knew could exist because it is a happiness none of us can ever know alone.

THE LIVES OF SAMUEL STEWARD

By the time Samuel Steward sat down to write his autobiography in 1978, at the age of sixty-nine, he'd had sex more than 4,500 times with over 800 different men. Each sexual encounter was carefully recorded in his Stud File, an alphabetically organised card catalogue that also, occasionally, included physical mementoes of his partners. There was a record for Lord Alfred Douglas, on whose body Steward's lips fell 'where Oscar's had been'. There was a card for Thornton Wilder, who lasted 'ninety seconds and a dozen strokes'. And there was one for the 18-year-old Ali, who was offered up by his companion, an ageing André Gide, in a room lit only by 'a frilly little pink tulip lamp'. The card for Rudolph Valentino, the Hollywood star, was augmented with a swatch of his pubic hair. There were records for almost every member of his high school basketball team, for many of the university students he taught as an English professor in Loyola and DePaul universities in Chicago, for what must have been half the sailors stationed at the Naval Training Centre on the shores of Lake Michigan in the 1940s and 1950s, and for the clients of the tattoo parlours Steward founded first in Chicago and later in Berkeley under the name of one of his many aliases, the tattoo artist Phil Sparrow.

The Stud File furnished valuable evidence for the pioneering sexual research of Alfred Kinsey, for whom Steward obligingly performed a sadomasochistic encounter that was recorded on film. It also provided material for the pornographic stories published under the pseudonym Phil Andros, tales whose erudite inventiveness had him hailed by Danish fans as an American Jean Genet. Steward was modest enough to dismiss such praise, but his pornographic novels did follow a more conventionally literary career that, before being derailed by alcoholism, had led to friendships and correspondences with Thomas Mann, Gertrude Stein, and Alice B. Toklas, with Steward maintaining annual visits to Toklas long after Stein's death in 1946. In *Everybody's Autobiography* (1937), Stein wrote that Steward's first novel, *Angels on the Bough* (1936), had that 'something in it that makes literature'. Although Steward ultimately wrote more than 20 books, ranging from social histories of tattooing to murder mysteries featuring Stein and Toklas as amateur detectives in Paris, he never got around to finishing his own autobiography, amassing a wandering manuscript that was culled to produce a series of disjointed episodes published as *Chapters from an Autobiography* in 1981.

This manuscript provided the basis of Justin Spring's 2010 biography *Secret Historian: The Life and Times of Samuel Steward,* and in 2018, Jeremy Mulderig combined unpublished episodes and published chapters to create *The Lost Autobiography of Samuel Steward.* To give this extraordinary gay life to the world, these books had to stitch together what Steward called his 'old artichoke heart'. He was 'in no case a sense of multiple personalities', he reflected, but 'the various pen names I used in the things I wrote, my Sparrow name as a tattoo artist and later the Andros name as a writer, were like the separate leaves that are capable of being stripped away'. 'But what', he wondered, 'was at the centre? The tough and dangerous inedible strings or the soft and delicate "heart" at the very bottom? Or perhaps there was nothing at all there, under any name whatsoever.' With nothing there, no authentic self underneath it all, perhaps Steward couldn't shape his many lives into a single autobiographical story. But maybe we don't need a single self or a coherent autobiography to be able to look back and say: I have led a good life. Maybe we don't need that kind of story to find happiness.

* * *

Samuel Steward was born on the 23rd of July 1909 in Woodsfield, Ohio, a small county seat close to the foothills of the Appalachian Mountains. It was a white Protestant town, flecked with 'Catlickers'. As a boy, Steward witnessed the Ku Klux Klan kidnap in broad daylight the father of

Woodsfield's only Black family, a chiropractor; his wife and children disappeared the next day. Cross burnings and Klan conclaves were common in southern Ohio. Woodsfield was isolated, yet the beauty of the surrounding countryside saw it christened the Switzerland of the state. Steward's mother died of an intestinal obstruction when he was six years old. His father was addicted to alcohol and prescription drugs and abandoned Steward and his sister Virginia to be raised by their grandmother and two maiden aunts in Woodsfield's respectable boarding house. These women were strict Methodists, lovingly devoted to Steward's education and powerfully repressive of any discussion of sex. His sexual awakening was provided by travelling sex education films by a friend Bill Shafer, who was memorialised by the coinage of 'shafering' to describe masturbation, and by a copy of Havelock Ellis's *Sexual Inversion* (1900), left behind in one of his aunts' rooming house bedrooms by a travelling salesman. Ellis provided reassurance that Steward was not alone in a world full of heterosexuals, as well a rich 'manual of the erotic' to guide his teenage years. Once he discovered what he wanted, Steward was certain of two things: 'that every corpuscle, every instinct I had, drove me unerringly in that direction,' and that 'no born-againer bigot is ever going to tell me that I had a choice'.

Woodsfield, Ohio, proved to be rich with opportunities for the teenage Steward to fulfil his sexual destiny – opportunities that, when seized, were strikingly without consequences. Direct propositions to members of the basketball and track teams, or to local toughs, were mostly successful. The local clock tower, graveyard and Methodist church provided easy to access venues. His forthrightness only caused him trouble when his father discovered that Steward left a note inviting a boarding-house guest to come and 'meat him' sometime. His father had to drive deep into the countryside before he could confront his son, who defended himself with the terminology of Ellis and the wit of Wilde. Not that his father's rage that his son might have been a 'cocksucker' bothered him – son had abandoned father as resolutely as father had abandoned son. His father died 20 years later of an overdose of booze and amphetamines. When his aunts moved their boarding-house business to Columbus, Ohio, so that Steward and his sister could afford to attend Ohio State University by living at home, the comparative metropolis of Columbus offered Steward riches memorialised in the poetry he began to write in imitation of A. E. Housman: 'Tis only right you look to wed / Now you are grown and gone / And I may comfort me to think / The lads come on and on.'

The sexual availability of ostensibly heterosexual young men was as remarkable as Steward's appetite. He never records being attacked or even that targets found his advances repulsive. This he put down to the protection of ignorance offered by Midwest American views on homosexuality. '[T]he fundamentalist mind made two breath-taking leaps of illogic: people did not do such things, and therefore such things must be non-existent.' The blessed illogic of Christianity protected Steward and his kind during the 1920s and 1930s; it was only when 'the audience grew more sophisticated did our danger (the knowledge of our actual existence) and our long ordeal begin once more'. Although he visited Greenwich Village in the 1930s, then the self-appointed centre of American gay culture under

Charles Parker and Henri Ford, Steward felt little need to migrate from country to city in order to live a full sexual life, the much-mythologised mainstay of queer autobiographies then and now, from Edmund White's *A Boy's Own Story* (1982) to Leslie Feinberg's *Stone Butch Blues* (1993). Given the extent of his some 300 sexual encounters in Ohio – by his own reckoning, Steward earned a total of 6000 years of incarceration at 20 years a head – his ability to find pleasure makes one wonder whether those generations of rural gay émigrés were really trying hard enough.

Columbus provided boys and bohemia enough for Steward, who continued at Ohio State to pursue a PhD in which he 'discovered' the homosexuality of Cardinal Henry Newman. Clarence E. 'Claire' Andrews, an English professor at Ohio State and friend of Stein and Toklas, introduced him to the world of modernist literature and the life of a prim and closeted English professor, the first of many surrogate scholarly father-figures whose sacrifice of sexual freedom for the price of academic acceptance would eventually result in their disillusioned rejection by Steward. Drifting into 'Bohemia in Columbus', a circle of bisexual artists living out their fantasies of garret life, brought Steward into contact with the poet Ben Musser, who provided an entry into the Stud File as well as a subsidy for the publication of Steward's first collection of short stories, *Pan and the Firebird* (1930). Even while he shuttled around the country after being awarded his PhD, taking remote teaching jobs in the midst of the Depression in West Virginia, Washington state and Montana, Steward continued to assiduously cultivate his 'telequeen network', a receptive web of mostly queer literary correspondents and holiday hosts: Stein and Toklas,

Gide and Wilder, Carl van Vechten, Thomas Mann and Paul
Cadmus. Steward showed an unusual persistence in literary
networking and autograph collecting – he discovered
the best way to get an author to respond to a fan letter is
not to ask them a question. Being gay enabled him to live
a particularly rich life in letters as compensation for that
restrained by law and social convention – and by syphilis,
picked up from a railway porter, necessitating a rare period
of enforced celibacy. Before the development of penicillin,
this required a gruesome cure: months of weekly injections of
arsenic, mercury rubbed into armpits, side-effects including
ulcers and purpura. Nothing more dates the writing of his
draft autobiography in 1978 than his breezy conclusion
that while syphilis wasn't especially traumatising in the
end, 'a great deal more care might be taken nowadays in
physical relationships if penicillin did not exist'. It's an idle
speculation about the impact of an incurable sexual disease
that would be impossible only a few years later, as AIDS
emerged to make Steward's autobiography the document of
an irreversibly lost way of sexual life.

A trip to Europe in 1937 enabled encounters with many
members of the telequeen network in the flesh. After a brief
visit to Housman's rooms in Trinity College Cambridge ('to
stand silently weeping, with chills along my spine'), the
first stop was the stuffy Regency flat in Brighton that was
home to Lord Alfred Douglas, whose face, no longer the
setting for Bosie's red-rose lips, had suffered 'the dreadful
slackening of flesh that comes with age'. Neither that
slackening, nor Douglas's strict and rabidly anti-Semitic
Catholicism, could prevent gin and bitters from doing their
work. Less memorable than the sex itself was the discovery

that Douglas only knew how to offer a 'shafering' since that is all he ever did to Wilde. From Brighton, it was off to Paris to meet Gide, who thoroughly disapproved of the dreadful Douglas. Living in Paris with his eighteen-year-old Arab companion Ali, Gide was more preoccupied with Europe's present, having just returned from viewing the face-off between the Soviet and Nazi pavilions at the 1937 Paris Exposition. By and large, the queer remnants of the modernist avant-garde hunted down by Stewart were holed up and withdrawn from history, like Wilder and Mann, who Steward encountered in Zurich. The former provided an unreciprocated entry to the Stud File that, nevertheless, didn't prevent Steward from becoming Wilder's 'Chicago piece' until the end of the forties. The latter was more reserved, yet obliquely confirmed what would only be revealed in his posthumously published diaries: that when it came to sex, *'Nihil humani a me alienum puto'*. Mann offered something for once more memorable than a fuck: a confession, as he put his arm around Steward's shoulder that '[i]t is through persons like you . . . that I hope to keep on living'. 'Of all the remembered gestures in my life', Steward wrote, 'that one is perhaps the most treasured.'

By far the most significant friends Steward made through his epistolary networking were Stein and Toklas, with a collection of their letters published in 1977. In 1937, the couple were living in Bilignin in southern France, where Steward returned for a second visit in 1939. Gertrude and Alice seemed as taken with Samuel as he was with them, and as well as offering praise for his first novel, *Angels on the Bough* (1936), they also gave him advice on how to develop a literary career. 'You can't write and teach,' Stein

admonished. 'The worst thing to do if you want to write is to
teach and here's why. You teach all day and then that word-
finding part of your brain is worn out and you can't find any
words to put down on paper because that part of your brain
is empty. It would be better yes much better to be a butcher.'
Steward, in turn, read and almost lost the manuscript of the
second volume of *Everybody's Autobiography* (1937). More
successful was his sourcing from the United States of the
couple's first Mix Master, whose arrival proved that nothing
was beyond Stein's inimitable style: 'Oh so beautiful is the
Mix Master, so beautiful and the literature [the instructions]
so beautiful and the shoe button potatoes that same day so
beautiful and everything so beautiful.' Having hurriedly
shipped out Steward and a hungover Cecil Beaton after a
visit in 1939 on some of the last trains not commanded by
the French military, Stein and Toklas stayed behind to enjoy
their American consumer gadgets as much as the regime
of Marshal Pétain, whose speeches Stein translated and
introduced. The ambiguities of Stein's politics were mirrored
by the ambiguity of her sexual identity: only once did she
ask, '[D]o you think Alice and I are lesbians?' If Steward
was happy to forthrightly declare himself what Stein called
'queer or gay or different or "of it" as the French say', Stein
never answered her own question. Generous to his idols,
for Steward, this was a sign of the generation gap between
himself and Stein, as well as Mann, Douglas and Gide: they
were 'really Victorian[s]' and 'more than a little reserved' in
terms of sexual identity as well as sex itself.

All this time, Steward was drinking. He had arrived at
Stein's reeking of Pernod. After the shock of seeing Stein
naked one night, he calmed himself with the emergency

cognac he always carried with him. He notes in passing that he was half-drunk when he climbed into bed with Wilder – 'as I had to be in those days to have an encounter'. By his own estimation, he was probably already an alcoholic when Prohibition ended in 1933, Ohio being well supplied with bathtub gin as well as gelatine capsules to coat the throat in order to make it palatable. His drinking increased during his wandering years as a precariously employed instructor of English to West Virginia farmhands and Montana cowboys. Steward blamed his turn to alcohol on the loneliness of being an academic – and his accounts of his drinking partners in academe show he certainly wasn't alone. But he does seem to have been one of the more extreme drinkers, relying on daily injections of vitamin B12 to get him through his teaching when he returned to Chicago in 1936 to teach in Loyola and then in DePaul University. Getting through a standard academic career while drinking a quart of whisky a day, as well as shots *en route* to class, would be perversely admirable enough if he wasn't also mastering a teaching range that would make the specialists of today turn to a drink themselves: 35 new courses in two years on topics from Anglo-Saxon grammar to the modern novel and everything in between, as well as courses in bibliography, linguistics and French.

The failure of Steward's academic career didn't come from a lack of intelligence nor from his alcoholism. He lost one job in Washington because his first novel contained a prostitute. He quit his job at Loyola in frustration with his Dean. He was fired from DePaul not for being gay, nor for his drinking, but for having taken up tattooing as a hobby from 1952 onwards: something that reveals as much about the morality of 1950s America as it does about the social history of tattooing.

Steward's own account of his alcoholism is oddly honest and obscuring at the same time. He called his years as an academic in Chicago in the 1940s his 'vacant years', so much so that he took to marking the calendar with crosses so that he could know what day it was and eventually ended up trying to commit suicide. Drinking cost Steward many friends, sexual and otherwise, but one who stayed with him was Emmy Dax, an older French teacher who Steward met through a pick-up who was staying for free with Dax and her grandmother in return for the vague hope that he would one day become her husband. After disabusing her of one closeted queer, Emmy fell in love with Steward, who 'in my own peculiar way' fell in love with her too (precisely 211 times). He bought her a wedding ring, became her common-law husband, broke her finger in an alcoholic rage and acted as her legal guardian and carer when the rare blood disease polycythaemia saw her confined to a nursing home for the last ten years of her life. And while he is unsparing in detailing the hurt he caused to others until, with the help of Alcoholics Anonymous, he became sober in 1947 and stayed that way for the rest of his life, he never notices the connection between his father's alcoholism and his own. Nor does he ever reflect on the fact that, during the years he spent cruising the sailors and salesmen of Chicago while performing a pastiche of married life with Emmy, all the sexual conquests he was otherwise so thorough in documenting took place while he was half cut.

Drinking, he confesses, took up 'the 17 years which might have permitted me to become a writer, a thing I

much wanted at one time'. Drinking also was one reason
that the autobiography he attempted to write remained
unfinished. 'At this distance from such a dark night of the
soul,' he concludes, 'I do not wish to recover in memory the
frightfulness of it; I have pulled down the window shade
and done my best to expunge it completely.' Here, again, is a
mixture of honesty and obfuscation. Those window shades
were drawn down long ago, for what is drinking but a means
to forget, an uncontrolled urge to leave parts of one's life
forever beyond recall? Long before he tried to write the story
of his life in the late 1970s, Steward's autobiography seemed
fated to remain unfinished, that very incompleteness as true
a record of his desires as the Stud File.

Why would such a prolific writer, obsessive record
keeper and unashamed exhibitionist be unable to complete
his autobiography? Why would anyone? Strictly speaking,
all autobiographies are unfinished. No one can write from
beyond the grave, so even those written close to death
leave out a portion of the life they purport to sum up in
words. Autobiographies are no less artificial than any other
literary form, but they might be more deceptive since they
promise a completeness they can't deliver. Steward might
have been, in the end, simply honest, unable to pretend to
write a definitive story of a life that remained incomplete.
Perhaps he was afraid. Who wants to risk, even at old age,
the finality of an autobiography: to admit that some stage of
a life is over? To make the decision, as he thumbed through
his Stud File, to finish with memory's endless potential to
refigure the past? Who would want to let go of everything
that is lost when you set down in writing that this is how it
was, this is who I was?

Still, he tried. He kept his records, he published his chapters, he thought there might be something there underneath it all. Perhaps the question posed by the contrast between his diligence in keeping his Stud File and his inability to finish his autobiography is whether we really need something there, underneath it all, to write a life story. Why couldn't that story be more like flicking through a card file: a series of snapshots to be selected at random and savoured without wondering or worrying who or what held them together? This would be an autobiography that took its shape from his desire: varied, accumulating, generous, addictive, insatiable. The choice to write about one's life reveals the self, at least for those who choose to make the attempt, to be an object of desire. You wouldn't seek to create it in writing if you didn't already possess it in life. In failing to complete his autobiography, at least according to a standard form because he felt he possessed too many selves, Steward was revealing something about how desire shapes our writing. Autobiography is a kind of monogamy.

Where does this leave those who want to write about Steward's life, those other passionate monogamists: his biographers? By writing about his life as if all the leaves of his artichoke heart could be laid out into the line of narrative, is the biographer's monogamy not fidelity, but betrayal? Perhaps of their subject, but not of their selves. Whether we go to the effort of writing, whether we pause over an unknown face in a photograph or whether we just dream about the dead: we want people from the past to give us their stories. We want these stories to give us models, scripts for living or warnings. We want predecessors, ancestors, a lineage. We also want mystery, incomprehensibility, a difference to define what we are. This is not the worst kind of wanting so long as we never forget that what we want is the story, not the person. We should own what we are willing to sacrifice in the pursuit of our desire. Or rather: who.

* * *

Getting sober was a turning point in Steward's life, one marked by the appearance of a new self: Phillip Sparrow, a monthly columnist from the years 1944 to 1949 in the *Illinois Dental Journal*. This name was lifted from 'a poem by John Skelton in the early 1500s [...] a Rabelaisian hodgepodge of buffoonery and erotic hints and much fresh charm'. Such indeed was what the good dentists of Illinois received from a correspondent who admitted to having been with Gertrude Stein 'in France in 1939 when it began to pop', who confessed a passion for collecting in order to 'escape from the present into the golden past, where we lie bound, gagged, and deliriously drugged among our souvenirs', and who ended an essay on male costumes asking: 'And tell me, dear, are my seams straight?' Up to a point, the journal's editors were like the Christians of Ohio, enabling a certain freedom through the blessed illogic of ignorance. They published some of his most insightful and vicious wit. In his essay on men's costumes, he analyses a man 'who join[s] the Ku Klux Klan, and in sheet and pillowcase, emblazoned with a fiery cross, combine[s] his innate sadism with the faecal symbolism of his dress'. Phillip Sparrow ultimately got himself fired – on purpose – by proposing that 'the South quietly secede from the United States', proving in the process that in 1940s America, a critique of white supremacy was far more threatening than blatant camp. But these columns – via a haughty takedown of Freudian psychoanalysis – saw him suggest that the masquerade of Phillip Sparrow allowed him to be more himself than the unified self-demanded by therapy: 'So I have sealed off my little room, and I will never open it to any psychiatric explorer who comes knocking inquisitively on a night of storm and tempest. [. . .] The only trouble is that I have to share the room with a guy who thinks he's Philip of Sparta. He's crazy, of course, because that's *my* name'.

This new self-provided the name for a new job. Steward got his first tattoo while appearing as an extra in a Ballet Russe de Monte Carlo production of *The Nutcracker* because it was the perfect addition of his 'role' as a gondolier. Tattooing seemed bound up for Steward with role-playing, providing him with a new identity as the Skid Row tattoo artist Phil Sparrow, and the time he increasingly devoted to tattooing, initially a hobby, offered a way out of the repressed hypocrisy of the Eisenhower-era professoriate and into a career that didn't require the strict separation of the sexual, the creative and the professional. It also paid much better: by 1954, 'my take from tattooing exactly equalled in one week what I made in one month of teaching!' The stakes of his decision to leave academia to become a professional tattoo artist are underscored by the fact that in his autobiography's account of this decision, Steward is also playing a role. There he describes having drafted a letter of resignation in advance of a meeting with his Dean because he intuited that he was going to be fired.

In his journal, as documented by Justin Spring in his invaluable biography, he records falling into despair after having been abruptly informed his contract is not being renewed because of his 'outside activities'. Steward preferred to see his decision as guided by another one of his many personalities, Edgar Allan Poe's 'Imp of the Perverse', forever 'turning me against my regimented life and making me burn intensely with a new hatred for all authority'. His role-playing in his attempt at an autobiography is a double shame since it seems to have distracted him from mentioning the only other tattoo he acquired: a series of inch marks running down his left arm so that he 'always had a hand a convenient ruler to measure objects in which he was interested'.

It was Steward's experience of tattooing, as much as his reading of Ellis and Gide, that taught him that homosexuality is the desire for the symbols of masculinity, not the man himself. Reflecting on his generation's attraction to the police, he laments that 'if cops could only realise how deeply attracted many of us are to them, they would never go horny again'. But they would have to wear their uniforms, since '[w]ithout the symbols of power, a naked cop would be just another naked body'. From here, it is not a great leap to the assumption that gay desire can be a kind of liberation since it reveals that masculinity is merely a costume. But there is a darker side to Steward's perception that a costume, rather than acknowledgement of a person, is often all that is required for the satisfaction of sexual desire. Satiation of lust and recognition of a common humanity can, in fact, be opposed, a truth about sex that goes beyond the experience of 20th-century gay men. Steward confesses genuine attraction for the hustlers he paid for sex, but only because '[e]ach of them fulfilled a fantasy of mine'. As is the case throughout this autobiography, Steward is a keener analyst of the sexuality of others than of his own. He turned to tattooing after sobering up and turning 40, a milestone when the 'male homosexual seems particularly vulnerable' to seeing 'his life disappearing behind and nothing but fog ahead, and he gets frightened'. Yet he only committed to it full time once he realised it was 'the most superb substitute for cruising that has ever been invented. If you become a tattoo artist, you will never have to go searching into the bars or baths again, for there you will find, as I did that . . . all the beauties will come looking for you'.

The closest he ever came to allowing someone else to analyse his sexual life came through his friendship with Alfred Kinsey, to whom Steward was introduced in 1949 by one of his many recurring sexual partners in Chicago. Steward became one of Kinsey's most valuable 'unofficial contributors' – university policy meant that Kinsey couldn't employ homosexuals even when, in Steward's eyes, he had done the most since Freud and Ellis to contribute to the liberating enlightenment of his century regarding sex. Steward fascinated Kinsey with his obsessive sexual record keeping, which for a time in the early 1950s extended to photographing his encounters on the newly available Polaroid camera and cataloguing the dozens of pornographic stories he had been writing and circulating in typescript among his 'friends'. Kinsey taught him never to use the word 'normal' in relation to sex and prompted the end of his sexual relationship with Emmy by simply asking, 'Why don't you stop?' It was also Kinsey who encouraged Steward to devote more time to tattooing and to investigating the sexual motivations of his clients. Steward documented '32 motivations for getting tattooed, of which 25 were sexual in whole or part'. For most, getting a tattoo was an assertion of masculine status – the only women he tattooed were the mothers of Hells Angels – one celebrated through masturbation as much as exhibitionism, gay or straight. Ever the record keeper, he noted that of those returning for their second tattoo, their first was followed by getting laid for 1,724, fighting for 635 and masturbating in front of a mirror for 879.

Only sporadically in his autobiographical fragments does Steward submit his own sexuality to scrutiny to try to analyse why he desired what he did. He admits that a 'fondness I had for the police was an indication, I suppose, of the deeply buried residue of guilt from my childhood which accounted for my psychic masochism', Almost grudgingly he allows that: 'One can never get entirely rid of these doleful shreds and tatters of the early impressments – in my case the stern and austere Puritanism of my Methodist aunts and my narrow upbringing.' Steward celebrated 'Freud as intuitive creator, Havelock Ellis as arranger and synthesiser, and Kinsey as scientist and investigator accomplished the liberating enlightenment of our century regarding sex'. Yet, at least in the writings he planned to reveal to the world, he appears by and large uninterested in enlightening the origins and reasons for the texture of his sexuality. He wanted to explore what desire could do, not wonder where it came from.

This reticence, this inability; this could be the price Steward paid for the pleasure obtained in life against odds that destroyed so many. Maybe he had to believe, as he said of his childhood, that he had no choice but to be as he was.

Maybe he had to think that he was submitting to fate. Maybe this was just the reality of what he experienced, as it is for so many. Was he too afraid, too ashamed, so he conjured up a vision of the self as ultimately unknowable and therefore alone?

We could also see this as an admirable refusal to the demand, as common among its professed sympathisers as confessed enemies, that same-sex desire has a cause: sin, childhood trauma, a pattern of genes. What do we want to know by knowing what makes us want what we want? To say we are born this way is to want to be seen as natural, but to say our desire is simply natural is also to evade responsibility: as if what we want isn't determined in part by the imperfect world in which we live. To show that we are made this way is also to show how we could be made differently: we could change the world, convert your soul, cure you through social conditioning and make you disappear. In Steward's professed lack of understanding, there is an unasked question: Why do our desires need a cause? Who wants knowledge of that cause if we can live well enough without it? Why do we even think of our desires as having causes, as having beginnings, middles and ends? Why, that is, do we think of desire as a story?

* * *

Approaching fifty, Steward was reborn again. After Phil Sparrow, the tattoo artist, came Phil Andros, the pornographic author. Alcoholism ruined one writing career, and his revelation, almost in passing, that he translated Genet's *Querelle de Brest* (1947) long before it appeared in

English as 'a labor of love', gives a sense of the talent that
was lost to drink. Yet by turning him to tattooing and the
steady stream of porn acts and producers that made up
his clientele, drinking ultimately brought him a second life
in letters. These clients led to his participation in another
network of correspondents, this time with the publishers
of early European gay magazines like *Der Kreis*, published
in Switzerland, and *eos* and *amigo* in Denmark. Under the
names of Donald Bishop, John McAndrews, Ward Stames
and Thomas Cave, Steward published analyses of 'The
Negro Homosexual in America', 'The Bull Market' (on
hustlers) and 'Pussies in Boots' (on leather fetishists), and
was soon encouraged by his editors to write pornographic
stories and to invent, in 1962, the character 'Phil Andros'
– an intelligent, widely read and sophisticated hustler,
'handsome as the rosy dawn', who was both a literary
character and authorial pseudonym.

Steward gave Phil the opportunity to romanticise the
hustlers he had known. He was observant and literate,
'with an unconcealed pleasure in the things belonging to
passion and gentleness for things of the intelligence and the
spirit'. Phil, in return, gave an ageing Steward the chance to
reimagine himself as someone else, depicted on the covers
his covers by the legendary Tom of Finland, a persona whose
measurements are as oddly precise as his author's Stud File:
'I'm a little over six feet with a 50-inch chest and 16-inch
biceps – and a good deal of hair on my body: a big triangular
fan on my chest, narrowing down to a thin line as it passes
through my navel, and spreading out again when it comes
to my prick.' Steward's pornographic writing tends towards
repetition, as pornography must do to bring pleasure, and

the best you can say about Phil Andros is that he gives his readers what they want. Yet amidst all the comings and groaning, there are flickers of social observation. When, in *Boys in Blue*, Phil temporarily joins the San Francisco police force, he notes that at the height of Gay Liberation, '[t]he fact remains that San Francisco leads in alcoholism, is second in suicides, and more psychiatrists per square inch than any other town'. And how many pornographic heroes can move onto their next fuck summoning the spirit of Milton's 'Lycidas' – 'At last he rose, and twitched his mantle blue, / Tomorrow to fresh woods, and pastures new'?

Pornography had been effectively liberalised in the United States after the 1966 Supreme Court ruling *Memoirs v. Massachusetts*, but tattooing was being increasingly restricted in Illinois, with a law requiring a minimum age of 18 destroying Phil Sparrow's business. And so, Steward packed up and set up another tattoo shop in Oakland, California. It was here, while living across the bay in Berkeley, that Steward became the preferred in-house tattoo artist for the Hells Angels. As they pass through his autobiography, Steward's tattoo clients offer a miniature history of changing American subcultures: from sailors in the 1940s to working-class street-gangs in the 1950s to the hepatitis-riddled hippies and Hells Angels of the 1960s. Tattooing became a replacement for cruising, but it also became a replacement for sex itself, in doing so revealing something about the passion that drove Steward's sexual life. Under the needle, customers voluntarily offered up the most unhindered confessions, so that 'for a little while I became for them wife, mother, best boyfriend, best girlfriend, priest, confessor, counsellor, and confidant'. The 'tattoo confession' offered the 'purest-kind of self-revelation, with all the faults exposed and the blame put squarely where it belonged – on the young man himself'. In tattooing, as much as sex, Steward discovered the self is most nakedly revealed when we submit to the control of someone else. Perhaps this is why, when turning to write his autobiography, exposed to no one but himself, he worried he would find no one underneath all the lives he had led.

* * *

In Berkeley, approaching his seventies, retired from tattooing, still finding himself falling for men, finding them becoming younger and younger, Steward saw himself faced with the problem of every ageing homosexual: 'In what year does a good man stop it all?' In the closing fragments of his autobiography, he wonders why 'I was never in love'. It was 'perhaps because I preferred a multifold experience rather than a long commitment to an idealized love object'. Each of his loves, each entry in the Stud File, 'answered some demand of my being or one of my different selves'. But he also wondered whether the fact he had never been in love was because he was 'intended to be solitary with such poverty of spirit that I could never enlarge myself to take in another? Was I too much an egoist?'

Just as the monogamist falls in love not with a real person in all their complexity, but with a person's capacity to sustain their fantasy, so too Steward wondered whether there was, in fact, a kind of selfishness underneath his desire to be the one who men confessed to, after sex, or in the tattoo parlour. 'The most dangerous of all egoists is the one skilled in what seems to be self-effacement, one whose outer kindness and gentleness really mask a complete and total centring on self, with a thorough indifference to others.' At the same time, when he was wondering about what lay under his artichoke heart, he was concluding that 'each man is an island, eternally sealed away from his fellows, whose mind-workings – even the simplest – he can never know. And no matter how much in love, in limerence, Everyman remains isolated and alone'.

Steward's sexual generosity seemed to be bound up with this intertwining of egotism and isolation. Not quite in the way that loneliness can drive you to use sex to give to others so that they will give you something in return, and thus to salve both egotism and loneliness, for a while, until the cycle repeats again. He believed that even if there was something or someone consistent across all the lives he led, it couldn't be shared with anyone else, and this enabled him to open himself more fully to the needs and desires of others. That he would leave a respectable if dull professor's job, that he would give up the drinking that got him through half his life, in order to pursue the tattoo artist's devotion to the bodies and confessions of other men shows the intensity of the pleasure this generosity can give. That he only really lived for others and was a closed-off island to himself suggests another reason why he could never finish his autobiography or at least never to a point where he was satisfied to publish it entirely and complete. If his greatest skill was self-effacement, if his greatest pleasures came from being with an ever-changing parade of others: for whom was this autobiographical self being called into being? If he thought some aspect of himself had to be closed so that he could be desired by another, maybe it is not so surprising that a paralysis might set in when writing for no one but himself. When he first moved to Columbus, he wrote that he went 'with the major purpose of bringing pleasure to others, mainly straight young men, and not to be concerned about pleasuring myself – for in bringing it to those I admired, I did please myself.' Decades later, an old man living in Berkeley, reflecting on why he wrote his pornographic stories, Steward wrote that he didn't do it for the money. Then as now, porn didn't always pay. Instead, he said, he wrote: 'To bring pleasure to lonely old men in hotel rooms at night'.

Writing, and all the imagination and fantasy it involved, was his gift to others. And yet, in giving that gift, he assumed – as the most dangerous of egotists would – that everyone was also as alone as he was. His imagination, so fertile when it came to sex, proved comparatively barren when turned towards the analysis of his self. It prevented him from seeing what others saw in him, what others could, in fact, know about the workings of his mind. When in his old age, Steward slept with a trio of triplets, one of them, Louie, told him: 'You seem to be a focal point around which so many lives revolve. Ours too. You'll always be there.' To which the only response Steward could record, perhaps the only one he could say to himself, was 'Hah!'

* * *

The Ohio schoolboy propositioning travelling salesmen. The friend of Stein, Toklas, Mann and Wilder. The alcoholic English professor. The abusive husband of Emmy Dax. The urbane columnist Phillip Sparrow. The tattoo artist to the Hells Angels, Phil Sparrow. The pornographic novelist, Phil Andros. Poe's imp of the perverse. Samuel Steward lived all these lives. And there were others that his autobiography passes over. The man who took hundreds of photographs of himself having sex with other men in the 1940s and 1950s. The sadist and the masochist who recorded himself on film for more men than Alfred Kinsey. The drunk who disappeared, wilfully forgotten, in his self-imposed vacant years. As with any autobiography, finished or not, the selves that appear in these pages are those he wanted to remember, those he wanted to be. What he wanted was to be various; he wanted to be them all. Or maybe he had to be them all; variety was no more a choice than his sexuality. To live even some of Steward's lives across the 20th century required an immense and life-long effort at compartmentalisation, the kind he described as sealing 'off my little room', which he will 'never open it to any psychiatric explorer who comes knocking' – not even to himself. That compartmentalisation might be pitied as collateral damage of living in the closet, a sad technique of survival left behind after the arrival of gay liberation. Yet if this is what led to such a rich proliferation of selves, it might be wrong to see them as compensation for a truer real life unwritten and unlived.

'What did I want?' This was the question he was left asking himself at the end of his life. It wasn't friends or love or even affection. 'I found myself wondering about happiness and the pursuit we make of it – so frantic and unceasing . . . the truth is that few men have more to their account than a total of a dozen hours of happiness in a lifetime – a fragment here and there out of the dull and sullen roll of years.' Whether from being spurned by younger lovers among the newly liberated generation of gay men in 1970s San Francisco or whether with the wisdom of age, he concluded that 'it is necessary to realize that a state of unhappiness or frustration is the usual lot of nearly all men, nearly all of the time. For most, life is a state of barely endurable discomfort'. The only cure was a kind of 'detachment', one that ensures 'no person or thing or situation would ever have the power again to wound'. This detachment, he counselled – and who was he counselling? – could be achieved by stockpiling one's inner resources, collecting 'a vast stock of tangible things to invest our love in: mementoes, memorabilia, photographs, an old blue cloak (like Newman), a water glass his lips had touched, anything which can stimulate us, can make us remember. And finally, when experience has multiplied itself to such an extent that you are no longer under any compulsion of any kind toward persons or things or situations, then you have the only kind of freedom worth aiming for, and the best reward.'

This, he realised, with age, was the purpose of the autobiography he had been keeping his whole life. 'The Stud File is full of cards and names and bits of coded information. The glass jar is packed with snippets of crinkly hair taken from my favourite persons, for when I was 17, I knew I was going to be 70.' Long before he knew what he was doing, 'I was getting ready for the days when the "island spirit" would be truly alone, without youth to visit me or to be ensnared – when the sort of happiness which Sophocles described might descend, the ultimate freedom from the "mad master" of sexual desire'. Yet his desire was the necessary pathway to that happiness, the only happiness he

believed you could know since sex provided those 'tangibles
to which the imagination and memory could be tied, devices
to stimulate nostalgia and the remembrance of things past'.
Sex as an act in itself may not have led to happiness, but it
provided the source of the memories whose recall, through
the imagination, provide the only kind of happiness he
believed in.

Perhaps to discover his own kind of happiness was the
reason Steward kept his Stud File. By failing to write the
story of his life as a straight autobiography, what we think
we need to give to others so that they can properly remember
us, Steward created a form of his own: all his scattered books
and chapters and essays, all those card files with their pubic
hairs. The very incompleteness of the record he left of his life
has allowed others to finish his story. To remember him in
their own way, so that he can become what they want him
to be, which is all we ever want from those with whom we
fall in love.

THE QUEER USES OF ART

In June 2018, I joined a crowd that assembled in Tate Britain to ask: 'What does a queer museum look like?' I lurked at the back, surrounded by the airless eroticism of Pre-Raphaelite portraiture, all drowning Ophelias and hieratic Lady Macbeths, while the founder of the Museum of Transology E-J Scott asked a mixture of queer activists and members of the public how to build a museum in which 'we can save the queer past for the queer future' and where 'we all can become curators of queer heritage'. For some, a queer museum was necessary so the world could see that queers exist. For others, a separate queer museum would only absolve other institutions from diversifying their collections. One member of the crowd questioned why Black queerness should be defined by a museum, itself a European institution long bound up with the colonial subjugation of Africa and its diaspora. There was little threat of the discussion getting out of hand among the Tate's polite, otherwise predominately white middle-class audience. But just in case, Scott had brought a box of children's plastic toy tools that he gave to those who wanted to speak. As the discussion developed, the toy tools were handed out one by one: a pink hammer, a green screwdriver, a blue spanner. Building a queer museum, Scott announced, was a matter of finding 'the right tools for the job'. I didn't raise my hand. This was a game I didn't want to play, at least not then.

A museum is an institution for relating things in time. It arranges objects not just in rooms but in a history that moves in a continuous line from past to present to show the development of a communal identity. In theory, this can be the universal humanity disingenuously imagined by the British Museum or the Louvre. In practice, it is often the more narrowly defined ethnic nation produced by Tate Britain, whose natural continuity and organic reproduction across time is enabled by the museum's presentation of an archive of 'our' past. Perhaps one reason why the discussion at the Tate had to be handled so delicately, as if disagreement was something that only happened among children, was because of a suspicion that as a way of using time, a museum is inherently contradictory with the idea of queerness, at least as it has so far been understood. Queerness is that which is opposed to what is natural, that which accepts genders and sexualities change across time and place, that which accepts the very idea that we have a 'gender' and 'sexuality' as historically novel, and really very strange, ways of understanding the self.

It may be that queer is simply what you make it, and that people might want a museum of queer art and history. And why not? No one should be begrudged the comfort of seeing themselves in the art of the past, so long as they recognise it comes at the cost of fixing a particular way of using that past – as a resource for the definition of an identity in the present. The very real danger that accompanies debates about what belongs in a museum, queer or otherwise, shows that the conflict about who and what goes in a museum is a conflict about who and what we are. That these debates seem so intractable is because using the past to create any identity inevitably ends up in an endgame of definitions: my past, your past; my museum, your museum.

But who is to say that any of this is what those who inhabited the past would have wanted? What might they have thought about being subject to the tools that build our museums, our identities? Maybe it would have brought them the greatest happiness, maybe the deepest horror. Probably most would have been mildly bemused. How often do we know how the dead would like to be remembered – or whether they want to be remembered at all? That we rarely stop to ask might be because we suspect, or at least aren't sure, that our desire for the dead to be our past won't be met with their desire for us to be their future, that behind the battles over institutions and identities lies a pathetic, unrequited love. Or it might be because to do so would force the question back on us, to make us think how we would like to be remembered, to confront us with our own impending death. That we rarely know what the dead want is a sign of how much we can forget, perhaps how much we need to forget, to put any kind of history to use in the present. But there are other ways of dealing with the past, ways that ask us to remember, paradoxically, that the past might not be very useful at all.

* * *

In 1992, Hamad Butt suspended nine sealed glass spheres containing chlorine gas from the centre of the roof of the John Hansard Gallery in Southampton. The spheres hung together in groups of three, like snapshots from the swing of a pendulum, creating the illusion of movement and a sense the glass might shatter at any moment and release the toxic gas within. In one corner of the triangular gallery, three-pointed glass tubes containing bromine gas were placed on top of metal poles that curved outwards and inwards as they ascended from the ground, the sharpened tips of a clenching claw. On the opposite gallery wall, ladders were installed whose rungs were glass cylinders containing iodine in a vacuum and an infra-red heating unit. A timer turned the heating unit on and off so that the iodine transformed back and forth from gas to solid.

Chlorine is an extremely reactive pale green gas at room temperature. If inhaled, it combines with water to produce hydrochloric acid and release nitric oxides so that the acid and oxides dissolve the lungs from within. Bromine appears at room temperature as a dark red liquid that evaporates into a gas of the same bloody colour. It does not produce an immediately visible reaction upon contact with human skin, and this delay makes it all the more dangerous. Inadvertently, the entire body can be exposed to damage, the skin later erupting with blisters and ulcers. Iodine is a lustrous violet solid that, when heated, transforms directly from a solid to a gas: a process known as sublimation. Although contact with skin in its pure state can produce irritation, iodine plays a prominent role in human medicine as it is a powerful disinfectant. It cures by killing.

These three chemical sculptures – *Cradle*, *Hypostasis* and *Substance Sublimation Unit* – made up an installation called *Familiars*, Butt's first commissioned solo exhibition. Born in Lahore, Pakistan, in 1962, Butt grew up in Britain and studied chemistry and physics, later graduating with a degree in Fine Art from Goldsmiths in 1990. Stephen Foster, the director of the Hansard Gallery, commissioned *Familiars* after seeing Butt's final year project, *Transmission*, exhibited at his graduation show. Like the tutors at Goldsmiths, who awarded Butt one of the highest ever marks in the history of the college, Foster told me that he thought Butt was a 'genius', albeit a shy and quiet one, and that *Transmission* expressed a darkly ironic view of life and death: 'People are attracted to things that destroy them.'

Transmission was an installation consisting of a vitrine, mounted on a wall, containing maggots and pages of text soaked in sugar solution. Over the course of the exhibition, flies were born from maggots, consumed the pages and died. This, Butt said, symbolised 'an endless cycle of information, literally eaten, and digestibly passed on'. The vitrine was surrounded by a ring of glass books, laid on the floor, text etched on their surface, illuminated by spines of ultraviolet light. 'Ultraviolet light is an invisible light', Butt said, 'a kind of invisible knowledge available in all knowledge but the closer you get to it the more dangerous it becomes [and] that's why . . . you then have to cross over to get the safety goggles to actually read the book.' The organic life cycle of natural reproduction destroys some kinds of knowledge rather than passing it on. The official knowledge that is archived in books, Butt seemed to be saying, was something of which we should be wary.

Transmission was later shown at Milch Gallery, which was founded in 1990, and which became a meeting point between London's underground queer scene and the generation of artists then graduating from Goldsmiths who would later be marketed as the Young British Artists. Butt's work was followed by the strikingly similar installation that first brought Damien Hirst fame: *In and Out of Love* (1991), in which butterfly pupa attached to canvas hatched, lived and died over the course of an exhibition. Ros Carter, a curator at the Hansard who helped install *Familiars*, remembers the 'extremity of the gay scene' centred around Milch. It was the height of the AIDS crisis; the style was 'overt and aggressive, tied into the S&M subculture'. There was 'a general culture of risk-taking and doing things to your body' that the art world began to share not only with the queer underground but also with the club scene, which by the early 90s was flooded by drugs. 'There were just a lot of chemicals going around, and a general air of toxicity.' Carter, however, had the sense that Butt didn't take part in the hedonism. He was 'a gentle soul, measured, reserved'.

In the texts written while creating *Familiars*, Butt wrote of his desire to explore what he called apprehensions: the 'seizure and arresting of perceptions' that we 'anticipate by fear to the point of understanding'. Apprehensions come after the biochemical processes corresponding to fear or stress. Fear and unease, Butt wrote, are 'understood, made comfortable, apprehended by the language that takes hold of this quality of experience'. He wanted to convey the apprehensions caused by the spread of AIDS: 'We cannot respond to this epidemic without fear and confusion, without aching to know why' and for the artist to 'legislate, so to speak, for the order of apprehending AIDS and the fear of AIDS . . . enjoins one to ironize the privileged role of the eye'. These apprehensions, at once so intangible and so consequential to those who acquire HIV, cannot be shown in a picture or described in writing. They are something more diffuse: a sense of poison in the air, of latent toxicity in the atmosphere, of fragile protection giving way.

A year after Butt died of an AIDS-related illness in 1994, *Familiars* was exhibited at the Tate in the group exhibition *Rites of Passage* (1995). Foster, who Butt had asked to publish his writings posthumously, remembers how, for years, the Tate refused to acquire *Familiars* for its permanent collection when it was offered to them by Butt's brother Jamal. Foster is certain that this wasn't due to institutional homophobia; rather, it came from a worry about 'how to preserve the toxic chemicals'. Butt, he remembers, took the risk less seriously: he used to sleep with the glass vessels under his bed. Eventually, after years of campaigning by Jamal Butt, Diego Ferrari, Jean Fisher and others, the Tate acquired *Familiars* for its permanent collection in 2014, although it has never been publicly exhibited. There is no doubt that museums fail to preserve the works of certain artists because of their assigned identity, but they also can fail to preserve the intentions of certain kinds of artists. Museums preserve objects, not atmospheres; things, not terrors.

In September 2018, the same samples of chlorine, iodine, and bromine that Butt sealed in glass in 1992 were taken out of storage and *Familiars* was reinstalled in the Hansard's new building in Southampton. The aim of the exhibition was to explore the curatorial issues involved in translating sculptural installations across time and place. Or as Carter, now Senior Curator at the Hansard, put it: 'Some things are made to be ephemeral, and you have to be careful not to restage things for the sake of it. If something is tied to a particular moment, there is a reason for that; you have to be careful not to be self-indulgent or to do it out of nostalgia.' Just as there is a tension between desire and danger at the heart of Butt's work, so too there is a tension in every act of curatorial reconstruction between the urge to do justice to a forgotten work and a cheap nostalgia that would betray it.

Hamad Butt might seem to be precisely the kind of artist long neglected by official art installations, whose work is now ripe to be recuperated within a queer art historical museum. As his story shows, however, such artists are never actually forgotten. They have always been remembered by curators, critics and other artists who have worked to achieve the mundane but consequential steps that, over time, lead to an artist's work enduring: publications, catalogues, purchases by national collections. Yet any attempt to use his work to build a narrative of queer art history – to use it to create an identity – is complicated by that work's own attitude to use. The desire to use this art from the past in a museum cannot overlook the fact that such works ask us to question what we want queer art to do and why we want it to do things for us in the first place.

Familiars doesn't just play with the expectation that art made by a queer person with HIV should be useful – a document of suffering recorded for the future. It also exaggerates its own use of these chemicals as a device to convey the atmosphere of fear surrounding AIDS in the early 90s. The pendulums only offer the illusion of movement; the glass claw only appears to clench. Butt noted that Susan Sontag's analysis of 1950s sci-fi movies showed that visions of apocalyptic destruction caused by fear of infection involve 'imaginative complicity with disaster'. 'The trauma of the body to which fantasy inures us is the opposition to collective nightmares that inspire a sense of humour.' To believe that a threat can damage you to the point of trauma is what gives that threat its power, and it is what forecloses other forms of resistance. Butt asked that the book containing these notes be accompanied by a hologram of the Bollywood actress Meena Kumari dancing in a scene from the film *Pakeezah* (1972). Kumari is one of the great camp icons of Bollywood, and in *Pakeezah*, she plays the role that distils why so many Indian gay men identified with her: a courtesan who hides her endless self-sacrifice in love behind a mask of decorum and who can only acknowledge her suffering by transforming it into an exaggerated melodrama of song and dance. Ever so subtly, Butt's writings camp the idea of art being used to convey the trauma of AIDS. *Familiars* takes unseriously the belief that art should be used to provide a historical document of queer suffering or identity and sends a message to its future viewers asking why we might want it to do so.

* * *

If I joined that crowd in Tate Britain not knowing what a queer art museum looked like, I did have a sense of what curators around the world believed would fill its galleries. In 2017, MOCA Los Angeles presented *Axis Mundo: Queer Networks in Chicano L.A.*, the first major retrospective of queer Chicanx artists, stretching back to videos of the

70s guerrilla drag performances of Edmundo 'Mundo' Meza and Robert 'Cyclona' Legorreta. That same year, the Museum of Contemporary Art Taipei was the first major institution in Asia to host an exhibition of LGBTQ Asian art: *Spectrosynthesis*. Although its focus was mostly on contemporary work, it reached back to include Shiy De-Jinn's 60s portraits of androgynous youths and Tseng Kwong Chi's *East Meets West* series of self-portraits (1979–89), anchoring the work of contemporary artists within a narrative of queer Asian art. Peter Hujar, whose composed monochrome portraits of Susan Sontag, Candy Darling, and Robert Mapplethorpe have shaped a romanticised image of downtown New York in the era before AIDS, has been the subject of retrospectives in Spain, the Netherlands and New York. Hujar's *Orgasmic Man* (1969), a photograph of a man's face twisted in the pleasurable agony of orgasm, provided the cover of Hanya Yanagihara's bestselling *A Little Life* (2015), implying that the novel's melodramatic saga of queer suffering was validated by belonging in a distinctively queer history of intertwined pleasure and pain.

Even exhibitions surveying contemporary art's preoccupations with gender and sexuality, like 2017's *Trigger: Gender as a Tool and a Weapon* at the New Museum, New York, saw artists like Josh Faught, Ellen Lesperance and Candice Lin preoccupied with archives of the queer past. Reina Gossett and Sasha Wortzel's *Lost in the Music* (2017) included Gossett's now rare footage of the Black trans activist Marsha P. Johnson; the question of who owns this footage became the subject of a bitter battle between Gossett and the producers of the Netflix documentary *The Death and Life and Marsha P. Johnson*, a sign that archives of queer history have been valuable commodities. Valuable and value-adding: the first exhibition shown at Peckham Levels – a redevelopment near where I live, 'bringing new life' (poké bowls, rented workspaces and white people like me) to one of London's major historically Black communities – was *Southwark QueerStory* (2018), a celebration of the borough's queer history that was promoted with a photograph from the 80s of a kissing Black and white lesbian couple. This area of London has fewer positive histories of race relations, such as those told by the poet Jay Bernard in their poem-sequence *Surge* (2019), which explores the 1981 New Cross fire in which 13 Black people died and which prompted mass demonstrations against the failure of the predominately white police to investigate the disaster. Evidently, these histories don't go as well with 'redevelopment' as images that instrumentalise queer love as the solution to racial oppression.

The desire for a queer archive has even seeped into the practice of living queer artists. In an interview about their photographic portraits of Black queers living in South Africa, Zanele Muholi has explained that 'I have created an archive that never existed in this country before'. For Muholi, if an archive of Black queer life doesn't exist, it must be invented: an identity can't be imagined without the contents of a museum. Karol Radziszewski, founder of the first Polish queer art magazine, *DIK Fagazine*, created the virtual *Queer Archive Institute* to host his collection of interviews, oral histories and magazines documenting queer life in Eastern Europe during the Communist era. Radziszewski wanted to preserve this material so it can be used for future artistic projects: 'everything that contemporary queer artists are doing is becoming a queer archive.'

For other artists, a queer archive is important only insofar as it can be used to imagine a different future. Paul Maheke's *A fire for a public circle* (2018), shown in Chisenhale Gallery in London, presented a daily performance whose background was a mural depicting a comic-book vision of outer space, a childish cosmology of distant galaxies. Each afternoon, Titilayo Adebayo and Heather Agyepong enacted a performance that restaged movements from performances by Bruce Nauman, Félix González-Torres, Eisa Jocson and Michael Jackson while reciting texts by Audre Lorde and Judith Butler, among others. Maheke wanted these performances to rearticulate 'pre-existing material, to rework it for the present moment': a process of 'queerness and blackness as modes of production'. Gestures were summoned from the past to create a 'space for reinvention and rearticulation' in order to 'think through identity outside of "identity politics"'.

For the Istanbul Queer Art Collective, founded by Onur Gökhan Gökçek, Seda Ergül and Tuna Erdem, performance and restaging are also central to queerness as a mode of production. Since 2012, they have enacted Fluxus performances in Turkey and elsewhere: performing the instructions left in the so-called 'event scores' composed by artists like John Cage and Yoko Ono. They do so to inhabit the perception, common in Turkey, that both contemporary art and queerness are Western imports. As Erdem and Ergül explain, 'being a lesbian is often referred to as something we have "copied" from the West.' They want these restagings and copying they enact to fail, not to 'fail better', like Beckett, as so to make use of failure – 'we just want to fail'. For Erdem and Ergül, queerness is an attitude to time: they want the failure of their restagings to produce 'transtemporal drag': to show what does not or should not translate across time. Their performances show the artifice of an assumed continuity between past and present and between the West and its others, just like the point of drag is to show the artifice of natural masculinity and femininity and to enjoy making it useless. These performances, like those choreographed by Maheke, felt like a different kind of archive to those I had seen documented in photographs and film on long museum walls. The particular archive summoned in each performance existed only to create something new in the moment, disappearing without being fixed into an authoritative canon. I felt temporarily part of someone's idiosyncratically assembled crowd, one as particular as the artists who had brought that crowd together.

The discussion at Tate Britain imagining what a queer museum might look like was organised in the aftermath of *Queer British Art 1861–1967* (2017), an exhibition that offered the closest Britain has to an official seal of approval for an archive of queer art history. Its wider historical range forced its curator, Clare Barlow, to confront an issue that other exhibitions of queer art, more focused on the recent past, could evade. The exhibition presented work from times when, as Barlow wrote, 'the modern terminology of "lesbian", "gay", "bisexual" and "trans" were unrecognised'. Neither was queer, but this was absolved of responsibility to historical accuracy. 'Queer' named past sexual identities 'that don't map onto modern sexual identities': Victorian and Edwardian artists understood themselves as 'Uranian', 'inverts' or members of a 'third sex', but certainly not queer. And yet, queer also named what these artists had in common with the contemporary notion of 'queer' as an oppositional sexual identity. The paradox of queerness naming something historically specific to the present as well as something continuous across time was shirked in the physical curation of the show, which moved in linear fashion, room by room, from the desires of the Victorian era to the explicit sadism of Francis Bacon in the 1960s. But this contradiction is not something that a different hanging, or even any museum, could: it is a paradox latent in the very concept of queer itself.

* * *

The freedom of queerness hits like a revelation: it doesn't have to be this way because it hasn't always been this way. Sex, desire, my gender, my body: these were different in the past and therefore, they can be different in the present. Few things are more convincing when trying to prove there is nothing natural about dividing the members of the human species into a hierarchy based on what they desire than being able to point, as Michel Foucault famously did in *The History of Sexuality* (1978), to the moment in history when homosexuality and heterosexuality were invented. The same move – using knowledge of the past to expose the myths of the present – frees you from believing that you are always only a man or a woman, that there are only things called men and women, that you will only ever desire one person, that desire is that important at all.

This leaves today's queers with a strange relationship to the past. The freedom of queerness is the realisation that the self and its desires are cultural, not natural: they change, and they have never been fixed. This means the queer can only know history in order to do without it, at least in any deep and extended sense. If selves and sexualities can be invented, then before a certain point, they didn't exist. Queerness is perhaps the most modern identity of them all, accepting of the most intimate aspects of our lives that all that is solid melts into air, all that is holy is profaned. Queers are cut off from the past by the revelation that sets them free. Queers need to do without history in order to be queer.

Queerness too was invented, which is to say that predominantly American and British activists, academics and artists participated in a collective decision in the 1980s to make 'queer' a term of communal identification and recognition. The paradox of queerness's relationship to history was acknowledged at its moment of invention. In the early 1990s, Judith Butler wrote that there was a tension at the heart of 'queer' as the name for an identity due to its being reappropriated from a shaming insult to a badge of pride. If, Butler wrote:

'the term "queer" is to be a site of collective contestation, the point of departure for a set of historical reflections and futural imaginings, it will have to remain that which is, in the present, never fully owned . . . This also means that it will doubtless have to be yielded in favour of terms that do that political work more effectively.'

The explosion of queer art and theory since the 90s was animated, maybe even defined, by this tension between queerness as a means of looking back and a way to imagine the future. As queerness has expanded beyond labelling a sexual preference to naming lives and communities that are not governed by the passage from childhood to childbearing or by the dictates and bonds of biological reproduction, queerness has come, for many, to be nothing so much as a way of living time outside the linear progress of history and the organic continuity of biological reproduction.

For Butler, at least in 1993, the potential of 'queer' as a political concept also lay not just in the refusal to ascribe it a fixed definition – something true in a banal way of any identity – but in the relationship it had towards time: a willingness to eventually abolish itself in favour of other, ultimately more liberating, ways of imagining selves and communities. If we remember that something is invented, we can imagine it ceasing to exist. We should remember what it means to be queer: that is, not to keep things the same, but to bring something different into being.

But what kind of memory is produced by an archive, a heritage, a museum? Part of Butler's hesitation about embracing queerness as a political identity came from the knowledge that, in the United States at least, earlier sexual identities like 'gay' and 'lesbian' gained political rights and cultural recognition only insofar as they modelled themselves on the ethnic identities of the Civil Rights era: Blackness, Asian-American, Chicanx. 'Queer' held out the promise of a different form of identity than 'gay' or 'lesbian': one that wouldn't be modelled on an ethnicity and would only use the past to imagine a different future – one in which queerness might cease to exist. Ethnic identities deserve civil and political rights because, or so the story goes, they name distinct cultures and ways of life, and the preservation of cultures is good in itself. Nothing more shows the distinction ⸢ ⸥ culture – and thus is worth – than the fact that it has ⸐ time and that there is a constantly renewing continuity between past and present. In an ethnicity, culture transforms back into nature, as in the imagination of one of the founders of this concept of ethnicity, the 18th-century German philosopher Johann Gottfried Herder: 'the Earth might be regarded as a garden, where here the one and there the other human national plant flowered in keeping with its own formation and nature.' National museums and archives are built to show the continuity of the natural species across history, which persists in a time modelled on biological reproduction. The first modern museums were museums of natural history; these are the forerunners of the art museums of today. They make each work of art the product of a natural species, bonded across time by the biological reproduction that queerness tries to escape.

It might be that the desire for a queer museum is just one moment in an oscillation between the idea of queerness being used to reflect upon the past and to imagine the future. It also might be true that, at least in the art world, the temporal tension at the heart of queerness has finally dissipated: it is no longer willing to admit the artifice of 'queer' as a sexual identity to the point of imagining its disappearance. It does seem that enough artists, curators, museums and viewers have decided that queers need the same kind of heritage as every other ethnic group in a liberal capitalist democracy to make this heritage a reality. Maybe they have realised that liberal capitalist democracies find it easier to grant rights to cultures than to redistribute wealth to classes. Maybe the thrill of knowing your identity is made up has come to feel hollow when faced with the solace of imagining your reflection in the past.

The attraction of a museum is that it holds an archive

of the past, ensuring that what could be forgotten will be remembered. But it also turns the past into a resource to be mined – with the right tools for the job – to create an identity in the present. To do so requires a particular model of time, in which the present is organically reproduced from the past, like seeds from a flower. In 2018, it was announced that London will get its own queer museum, and in time other cities around the world will too, producing a global archive of what it means to be queer. Just as the museum spread from Europe to the rest of the world, so too a certain memory of queerness will probably spread to Taipei, Mexico and Johannesburg: drag, vogueing and dykes, but not hijra, mashoga or two-spirit. Different ways of using the past will continue to exist, ways that make useless notions of continuity modelled on nature; they might continue to be recognised as queer, or they might lead to other political practices and collectivities.

There is nothing inherently revolutionary about novelty. The proclamation of being without precedent sounds a lot like the slogan of a new product for the market. We need to remember to preserve some important truths. People suffered in the past for desires, touches and glances that today seem so casual you forget how much they mean. People suffer today for the same reasons, and there is something obscene in how posters appear in London and New York celebrating that HIV can be untransmissible simply by taking one pill a day while hundreds of thousands continue to die of AIDS in Africa and Asia in a pandemic most of the world seems to have forgotten.

And perhaps this is the deepest reason behind the longing for a queer museum for all its faults. So many lives have been forever cast into oblivion because of nothing more than what someone wanted and who they wanted to be. The institutions that might preserve the memory of those on the cusp of disappearance in our own time, whether the entire generation lost through AIDS or those suffering under the state-imposed neglect of trans life, barely exist. But if these people are remembered only in order to tell you who you are and to construct a spectacle of continuity to be presented to the public, it's a question of whether their difference is really being remembered at all.

* * *

The opening night of the exhibition of Butt's *Familiars* was attended by members of his family: his parents Jamilia and Masood and his brother Jamal, who, in a conversation afterwards, told me that he stored the glass vessels that made up the installation in his attic in his house in North Finchley in the years before the work was bought by the Tate. When he found out I had spent months researching Butt's life and work, Jamal told me he thought Hamad would have found it funny his work was being taken so seriously so many years later. Hamad had such a sense of humour, Jamal remembered. He loved that when *Familiars* was first exhibited, the gallery made it seem more dangerous than it was by hanging gas masks and asbestos suits in the foyer for visitors to use, even though they weren't necessary.

If a museum might not be an institution that can achieve the paradoxical task of preserving the memory of the past in order to bring a different future into being, neither can today's queers always rely, like Butt, on the institution that is the family. One reason I spent so long researching Butt's life, interviewing curators and trawling through the archives of the Goldsmiths College library, wasn't just because I felt less at home in that earnest crowd assembled in Tate Britain than one I imagined, back in the 1990s, in which Butt laughed, with elaborate care, at my attraction to knowledge, my desire for memory, reminding me that too much of both might be poison, might not be the path to happiness. It was also because his were desires, sensibilities and lessons that had not been passed down through my family, which could not have been passed down through any straight family, and probably never will be in the future. The queer family exists, but what it might be able to remember, and preserve is, for now, as uncertain as that which might be achieved by a queer museum. And this is why art and literature matter, why the question of how they are preserved matters, why I turn to them to assemble a crowd, not a family, of my own. They are one way that memories of others can be passed on outside the biological family, even if what those others might want you to remember is that they didn't just exist in order to be remembered by you.

In 1952, Jean Genet wrote to Jean-Paul Sartre: 'In any event, the significance of homosexuality is this: A refusal to continue the world. Then, to alter sexuality. The child or the adolescent who refuses the world and turns towards his own sex, knowing himself that he is a man, in struggling against this useless manliness is going to try to dissolve it.' For Genet, the homosexual's refusal to continue the world was also a way to make parts of that world useless. He idolised not the organic reproduction of the natural world, but the flowers he imagined that bloomed from being spat upon, and that wreathed his drag queen Divine: artificial roses not living flowers. The idea that a sexuality is not a definition you identify with, but a way of taking pleasure in making things useless, is neither specific to Genet nor to the identity of a 'homosexual'. It is what drives the spectacle drag kings make of the masculinity normally used to subjugate women. It is what enables the pleasure of camp, which delights in what is outdated. It is what marks any person whose desires aren't tied to reproduction: from the point of view of evolution, they are simply useless. Queerness as a practice, rather than an identity, and can be a way of being comfortable with being useless. It can be a way of remembering the past that refuses to continue it – a way of seeing the past for what it is for the very first time. It can be a way of growing out of the family you find yourself born into since for all that queers might want to refuse to continue the world through reproduction, none of us can escape being born.

A museum of queer art would ensure that the past will not be forgotten, but we should never assume it is the only way of remembering the past. Nor should we ever assume that it makes the past familiar. We call things familiar when we think we know them well, as if they were members of our family. The word assumes that we are most at home with the people who made us, that we are most comfortable with what is natural, and that the belief we know how to use something is akin to it belonging in our family. Yet familiars are also the animals that assist practitioners of magic. They appear only to enable the essence of magical thinking: that pretending makes it true. When people cast spells in our disenchanted world, they know that crystals are useless for healing wounds, that dancing doesn't make it rain – they just pretend these things are useful in order to imagine changing the world around them. We shouldn't forget, as Butt wrote of his *Familiars*, that art can do more to make the past as familiar as if it were a member of our family. It can also make that past conjure up something new: 'There is the acknowledgement of loss and the numbness of its repetition, which moves us in particular to displace fear with some kind of charming dialogue; an ungraspable sleight of hand.'

FEAR OF A GAY PLANET

In Robert Ferro's novel *Second Son* (1988), Mark Valerian suffers from an unnamed illness afflicting gay men, spread by sex, and for which there is no cure. Mark's only hope seems to be a medical trial that requires the transfusion of white blood cells genetically identical to his own, until his friend Matthew, who recently lost his lover to the 'Plague', begins writing letters to Mark revealing another potential cure. Shortly after the 'Plague' erupted some seven years ago, a group of gay men made contact with aliens living on a planet called Splendora, who are 'long, lean, delicate, in the sense of a swimmer's body'. 'Darling,' Matthew writes, 'they *are* gay.' The aliens' advanced technology promises to enable a group of gay men to escape to Splendora, be cured of their illness and live safely on a planet populated only by gay men – and gay aliens. Mark dismisses Matthew's letters as the fantasies of a dying 'queen out of control'; his family eventually acknowledge his illness, and a brother donates the blood needed for his trial. Yet the novel ends with Mark and his lover Bill gazing at the sky, 'waiting as if for the ship to Splendora', attracted, despite themselves, to Matthew's fantasy of a gay planet. It was a fantasy that seemed to promise everything: freedom from homophobic hate, a cure for the 'Plague' that doesn't require gay men to fall back on the genetic identity of the biological family, and the certainty that gay life will survive forever. There is, however, one detail that Matthew couldn't explain about how the gay planet sustains itself across time: how it creates new generations of gay men that will inherit and continue the legacy of Splendora. 'Reproduction is something of a mystery.'

How is gay life reproduced? Should gay life be reproduced? It is, after all, just one historically specific interpretation of the body and its desires and a far from uncompromised one at that. But still, it has its joys since it enables, sometimes, those desires to be satisfied like nothing else on this or any other planet. What is Matthew dreaming of beyond being cured of the 'Plague'? It isn't eternal life, for, fabulous as Splendora may be, that isn't something it offers. But Matthew doesn't fear death. He fears what will happen to his lover, disowned by his family, or to Mark, whose parents won't even acknowledge his illness. He is afraid of being forgotten. For so many gay men of his generation, and so many queer people today, biological reproduction is not the means by which his way of life will be passed on, which is another way of saying it is not the way some parts of that gay life will be remembered. For how could it? Even in his dying fantasy, how gay men can have gay children remains a mystery. And yet the fantasy of reproduction, of the biological family as a means of creating someone whose mere existence preserves your memory after you die, is so powerful that it leaves Mark and Bill staring at the stars, wondering what it might be like to make their fantasy a reality.

While Ferro's novel leaves us wondering, it is telling that even in suggesting that a gay planet might be possible, it touches on the imaginative powers of science fiction. For centuries, writers, artists and speculative thinkers have used science fiction to imagine the possible futures we might have. That's one reason the genre has long been a storehouse of fantasies about reproduction. Imagining a different future requires imagining a different way of getting there, and the way we get there, the way any group makes it to any future, is by reproducing itself over time. Science fiction's reproductive fantasies have rarely been utopian in any simple sense since one group's utopia can all too easily slide into another's dystopia. But because of the genre's commitment to world-building – its requirement to have, if not always directly reveal, a logical and technological explanation for every part of its imagined world – it requires writers to explain how their fantasies of the future can be made real. Sometimes, such world-building can be lazy, gesturing towards a logical explanation for its fictional world without ever convincing the reader. In other cases, it can be almost neurotically belaboured. Those extended histories of alternative galaxies, chapters outlining the reactions of alien chemistries: tedious as they may be to read, they show the amount of work that has to go into imagining a different future, and how important it is – for the characters, as much as the authors – that they remember how their worlds came to be.

These exercises in world-building are ruled by the science available to the writer, even if they move beyond it: the extent of an era's science forms the horizon of its science-fictional possibilities. And that is why science fiction's reproductive fantasies never only belong in their alternative futures but in each writer's present: its knowledge, its politics, its desires. Science fiction forces characters like Ferro's delirious 'queens out of control' to take their desires down from the starry skies of fantasy into the grey prose of reality. It makes these dreamers answer the hard questions lying behind any dream of a gay planet. Can gay desire only survive when gay men are able to control their own reproduction? Should we desire a gay planet at all? It's easy to mock these intergalactic fantasies, as Mark does. But just as science fiction is never only about the future, the planets it creates are born out of desires we can find, now, on this planet of our own.

* * *

Gay men in the 1980s, living under the shadow of AIDS, were far from the first to imagine a world where reproduction happens beyond heterosexuality. One of the earliest feminist science fictions, *Mizora* (1890) by Mary E. Bradley Lane, is also one of the first outlines of a completely self-sustaining society populated only by women. In the novel, the women of Mizora have reached a level of scientific progress where they can reproduce life in laboratories and have chosen to eliminate men, the source of all war and violence. They have also eliminated 'idiots' and 'lunatics' and all but the 'fair race', since, as one of their leaders, the 'Preceptress', puts it, 'the elements of evil' – stupidity, greed, and a lack of 'genius' – 'belong to the dark race'. That certain feminist aims could be achieved by eugenics was no mere speculative fantasy. Many commentators at the turn of the 20th century, from Bradley Lane to the birth-control activist Marie Stopes, were convinced that the promise of technological progress would not only enable women's liberation but would also improve the health of the human race. It turned out that this improvement involved ensuring that vigorously able European bodies could continue the projects of colonial rule and imperial settlement, revealing that for these feminists, the 'human' race was ideally a white one. Another such society, discovered by three male explorers, appears in Charlotte Gilmore Perkins's *Herland* (1915). The women of Herland reproduce through parthenogenesis or 'virgin birth'. Much like in Mizora, they are all 'of Aryan stock', practicing 'negative eugenics' by disposing of 'bad types' at birth: bodies that function differently and are racialised as dark, black and brown.

In the century since *Herland*'s publication, science fiction has built countless worlds where new life is created outside a biological interaction between a man and a woman. Some of these are worlds beyond gender, as in Marge Piercy's *Woman on the Edge of Time* (1975). In Mattapoisett, a village on a future version of our Earth, genetic material is held in communal laboratories and used to create embryos in 'brooders' or external artificial wombs. Gene samples are intentionally mixed to eliminate racial difference and, because reproduction takes place through technology, gender distinctions no longer exist, with residents of Mattapoisett defining themselves as 'pers'. Others feature coupling between humans and aliens, as in Octavia E. Butler's trilogy *Lilith's Brood* (1987-9), in which a race of Oankali are able to mate with humans, and any other species, by means of their own biochemistry. Butler's suggestion – implicit in her heroine Lilith's Blackness, explicit in the way the Oankali breed humans the way humans breed animals or the way white slavers bred Black slaves – is that what we call 'the human' is not just a biological fact or philosophical ideology, but a fungible concept we use to negotiate the limits of reproduction.

Since second-wave feminism of the 1960s, several novels have introduced meticulously described societies consisting only of women. Rather than seeking to transcend gender, these worlds reflect a belief that only female separatism can end patriarchal control over women's bodies and over the process of social reproduction those bodies enable. In Joanna Russ's *The Female Man* (1975), the planet Whileaway is populated exclusively by lesbians, all men having died in a plague centuries ago. They use microsurgery to splice together two eggs and impregnate willing carriers with the resulting embryos, enabling conception and birth to take place without men. On Shora, in Joan Slonczewski's *A Door into the Ocean* (1986), a race of women called Sharers create new life through a 'fusion of ova' enabled by 'lifeshaping', a form of genetic engineering. Sharers are innately peaceful; men, or Valans, are innately violent, and the novel is built around a series of similar gender binaries. These planets are fantasies twice-over: a fantasy that reproduction can take place without men and a fantasy about the success of

female separatism. Female separatists of the 1970s argued
that all forms of heterosexual relationships were inherently
oppressive, and that liberation could only be achieved in a
society free from men. Or, as the slogan went: 'Feminism
is the theory; lesbianism is the practice.' Yet, these worlds
notwithstanding, one kind of planet remains as rare as it
was when the inhabitants of Herland asked the Edwardian
adventures who found them: 'Have you any forms of life in
which there is birth from a father only?' 'I know of none,'
replies our explorer, Terry, 'and I inquired seriously.'

One such planet is imagined in Lois McMaster Bujold's
Ethan of Athos (1986). Set in a distant future, Athos is a planet
exclusively populated by gay men, settled centuries ago by
a group of Founding Fathers, who came to believe that only
a separate planet could protect gay men from persecution
in a homophobic universe. The Founding Fathers settled
on Athos with a batch of ovarian tissue and the ability
to grow embryos in artificial wombs to ensure that only
men are born. The Founding Fathers expected Athos to
grow by attracting gay immigrants fleeing oppression,
but immigration soon slowed, and, at the opening of the
novel, it is revealed that the original ovarian tissues are
about to stop producing eggs. The only solution is to send
the novel's hero, Ethan Urquart, out to buy new tissue on
the intergalactic black market. After his first purchase is
mysteriously sabotaged, he heads to a trading post where
he meets his first-ever woman – 'uterine replicators with
legs, as it were' – Commander Elli. Elli is a spy intent on
unravelling the mystery of Athos's sabotaged shipment, and
they develop an unlikely friendship. Ethan is astounded
to learn that on other planets, unlike Athos, parents are

not compensated for the work they do raising children. It's 'counted as free', Elli tells him, 'they call it women's work.' Bujold uses Athos to illustrate one of the key claims of the Wages for Housework movement: in capitalism, the reproductive capacity of those who reproduce is a form of exploited labour. But the implication of this strange alliance of Marxist feminism and gay separatism remains uncertain. If people were compensated for their reproductive labour, a capitalist economy might not be able to generate a surplus and would collapse. Is the solution to eliminate capitalism – or, as in Athos, eliminate women?

Elli helps Ethan unravel the mystery of the sabotaged shipment. A military project on the planet Cetaganda tried to breed humans capable of telepathy, but only one survived, Terrance Cee, who switched the shipment Ethan was meant to receive, so it contained an ovary containing telepathic DNA. He hoped that if this ovary reached Athos, it would spread safely since it would be the only set of female genes used on a planet with no other women, producing as a byproduct a race of gay telepaths. Terrance's scheme, however, was foiled when a woman whose gay son had fled to Athos sabotaged his shipment in order, as he puts it, to 'cut you unnatural motherless bastards off' – exemplifying the homophobia that remains in the universe outside Athos. In gratitude for Ethan's help, Elli donates an ovary to Athos, but with the knowledge that it too will eventually stop producing eggs, and Athos will need to search for new ovaries all over again. At the last minute, Ethan realises the benefits of Terrance's plan: if all gay men became telepaths, they could use this power to safely steal ovaries from the rest of the universe in perpetuity. He sneaks the telepathic

DNA back to Athos and raises a family with Terrance, who reveals a hitherto secret attraction to Ethan and becomes his 'designated alternative', that is, his husband, and they plan to have a gay child of their own.

Bujold's novel might seem like a bizarre, niche fantasy, but it addresses a real problem. What happens if gay men think the only way they can preserve gay life is through creating their own separate society? The plot pushes this question to its limit, leaving Ethan faced with a dilemma: accept that reproducing a gay planet depends on the generosity of women in a way he can never control, thus failing to become fully self-sufficient and independent or attempt to maintain a separation that places his gay planet forever at war with women, condemned to launch raiding parties to steal new ovaries every couple of hundred years. To preserve a gay planet, he believes: 'There are only two choices in the long run that don't risk race war or genocide: all, or nothing.' In the end, Ethan chooses Terrance's mutant telepathic ovary. He chooses all, he chooses purity, he chooses war.

* * *

Ethan's dilemma isn't just a plot twist in an obscure science fiction novel: it runs throughout the unconscious of modern gay identity. Gay identity – in distinction to identities like the homosexual, the poof, the sissy or the queen – was born out of the counter-cultural movements of the 1960s, from which the gay liberation movement borrowed some of its more radical beliefs. One of these was the idea that gay culture, and indeed gay people, could only survive when separated from a predominately straight society. In 1969, Don Jackson

of the LA Gay Liberation Front proposed that hundreds of
gay men should move to the sparsely populated Alpine
Country in the California mountains and set up 'Stonewall
Nation' as a 'Gay Homeland'. Plans advanced far enough
to consider strategies for gathering gay children from state
institutions and care homes across the US, thus relieving
the government of a financial burden. The organisers also
considered sending diplomatic contacts to gain recognition
for their new state from the Algerian government, which
at the time also provided a haven for Black Panthers like
Stokely Carmichael in an attempt to undermine what it saw
as American Cold War imperialism. 'Stonewall Nation',
according to Jackson, would be an exclusively 'Gay territory'.
Like Athos, he insisted, the colony 'could become the Gay
symbol of liberty, a world centre for the Gay counter-culture
and a shining symbol of hope to Gay people in the world.'

The Alpine Country project ultimately failed: the largely
Christian existing residents refused to sell their land, and the
once-keen gay activists blanched at the thought of camping
out in the mountains all winter while waiting for a chance to
buy property. However, the belief that a separate gay state
was the only way to secure the preservation of a newly self-
defined gay people was, if not widespread in the 1970s, not
exactly marginal either. In 1989, Larry Kramer, the AIDS
activist and founder of Act-Up, saw the state of Israel as a
model for gay liberation. 'For a while, San Francisco was the
gay Israel . . . Tragically, with the devastation of AIDS, gay
power in San Francisco has waned considerably. We don't
have Zionism as a hopeful haven from the world's hatred
of us.' Kramer believed that gay men during the AIDS
crisis were like Jews during the Holocaust, threatened with

extinction by a hostile world. In his call for a gay state, he invoked Hannah Arendt's description of the threat that was facing Jews: 'As Arendt pointed out, Zionism's solution was not one of fighting anti-Semitism on its own ground, that is, wherever it existed, but to escape it . . . "The simple truth is that Jews will have to fight anti-Semitism everywhere or else be exterminated everywhere'."

Arendt's argument was the opposite of what Kramer thought it was: writing in 1946, she warned that a separate state would not protect Jews from anti-Semitism and that, in fact, it could weaken the commitment to eradicating anti-Semitism by implying that all one had to do to escape it was to move to Israel. Perhaps Kramer's mistake was caused by the pressure of the AIDS crisis at its peak, perhaps by political expediency: 'Israel' being a metaphor for an acceptable form of separatism. Perhaps it was caused by a willed ignorance to the sufferings of others, not just those who suffered due to the establishment of the state of Israel, but to those neither gay, nor male, nor white, who also suffered – and still do – the devastation of AIDS, and who presumably would find no hopeful haven in Kramer's gay state. Undoubtedly, Kramer's desire for a gay state involved blindness to the specificity of Zionism as a response to anti-Semitism. Instead, he saw a model where a way of life became an identity that, in turn, became a people requiring a state to protect them. Otherwise, that people would become extinct, and, as was also the purpose of the Holocaust, the rest of the world would forget they ever existed.

In the 1970s, William Burroughs also took Zionism as a model for the solution to gay oppression, a view that similarly collapsed it into a vision of a separatist state. He

reflected in an interview that: 'Now that we've been forced
into the same position of Jews, perhaps we should enact the
same strategy. We should try to get our own state like Israel
. . . I believe that Gays should be allowed to live in an all-
Gay community.' If this didn't happen in reality, Burroughs
imagined it in his 1971 novel *The Wild Boys: A Book of the
Dead*. The wild boys of the title are an ultra-violent, knife-
wielding, jockstrap-wearing horde of gay men who live
in the deserts surrounding Marrakech. This was not quite
the Marrakech nor the Morocco where, like writers from
André Gide to Jean Genet to contemporaries including Juan
Goytisolo, Burroughs had pursued a desire that fetishised
the racial difference of the 'Arab': as more masculine, less
rational, and always available for purchase. 'Marrakech',
like the 'Interzone' that appears in Burroughs' novels like
Naked Lunch (1959) and *Nova Express* (1964) as a fictional
territory outside the control of any centralised state, here
offers a vision of future capitalism: an imperial city-state
dominating the surrounding natives, whose white populace
consume drugs, violence, and technologically mediated
sexual pleasure while the world around them suffers
ecological collapse. It's not clear whether the wild boys are
resistant to or complicit with the violence of Marrakech.
Their gay separatism exiles them from the city's pansexual
pornocopia, which encourages its inhabitants to pursue
endless new pleasures in order to endlessly sell them new
products. It forces them to become murderous killers as they
fight the violence of the city's authorities with violence of
their own. But their gay separatism also provides a unifying
principle that transcends the racial divisions of empire: the
wild boys are made up of men of all races. Less a separate

gay planet, in Burroughs's imagination they are like a virus spreading within our own: 'the wild boys exchange drugs, weapons, skills on a worldwide network.' At first, the wild boys reproduce by finding surrogates on the black market: 'A baby and semen black market flourished in the corrupt border cities . . . You could take your boyfriend's sperm to market, contact a broker who would arrange to inseminate medically inspected females.' Then, in 'clandestine clinics, fugitive technicians experimented with test-tube babies and cuttings', attempting to grow embryos in male assholes. But eventually, the wild boys transcend science to create offspring known as Zimbus. In ceremonies that take place during vast orgies, men conjure 'mist' out of the sky that becomes a 'phantom' boy that they then fuck until they cum inside the phantom, and it suddenly becomes real, steaming flesh. When families watching *Top of the Pops* in the 1970s sang along to Bowie's 'Ziggy Stardust', whose appearance was modelled on that of a wild boy, or when countless bros pumped iron to Duran Duran's *Wild Boys* in the 1980s, the virus of Burroughs's gay separatism was spreading via generations of dumbly oblivious heterosexual hosts.

As a response to homophobia and as a way of ensuring gay life is preserved across time, gay separatism might seem today to be a forgotten relic of 1970s radicalism. It was overshadowed first by the crisis of AIDS when gay men had to fight for support from actually existing states to access the medical treatment they needed to survive, and then by the emergence of queerness as a theory, practice and identity that denied any fixed separation between different kinds of desires. But its legacy can be detected in what might appear, at first, to be a wholly unconnected movement increasingly dominating 21st-century politics. Gay men play a puzzlingly prominent role in contemporary white separatist parties. In the 1990s, Pim Fortuyn in the Netherlands and Jörg Haider in Austria began Europe's turn to racist populism; by 2017, a third of French gay men said they would vote for Marine Le Pen's Front National. The belief that 'white' people will become extinct due to the higher rate at which other 'races' reproduce is one of the rallying cries of white supremacists around the world and is often called the coming 'great replacement'. The term was first coined by the French writer Renaud Camus in the 1990s and subsequently outlined in books such as *Le Grand Remplacement* (2010). But Camus' fears of white extinction first appear, decades earlier, in the unlikely pages of a book called *Tricks* (1979), which chronicles the casual sexual encounters between men that have been made possible by the new world of gay liberation. For Camus, what liberates his generation of gay men from shame is that they transcend the division of tops and bottoms, roles which, for Camus, serve to mimic the hierarchy of heterosexuality. If you top in the morning and bottom at night, then gay sex becomes the great equaliser, and freedom can be achieved by fucking.

For Camus, one group threatens this new sexual utopia: 'Mediterraneans', a euphemism that really means the North African men who emigrated to France after the Second World War. 'Mediterraneans', he argues, remain trapped in 'a sexuality of roles, rigorously defined once and for all'. They distinguish between objects of desire not in terms of gender but in terms of a hierarchy between tops and bottoms, valorising the former and denigrating the latter. In Camus' imagination, the problem with 'Mediterraneans' is that they bring this hierarchy and its attendant shaming into the otherwise proud orgy that modern gay life is meant to be. The 'Mediterranean' man has a different kind of sexuality: the implication is that he can fuck both men and women in a way that the white gay can't, threatening white gays in France not only with shame but with the prospect of being outbred by more virile North Africans. Some 'Mediterraneans' may fuck men, but all will at the same time be fucking women, thus reproducing at a faster rate than white people, an increasing proportion of whom are gay men opting out of having sex with women. According to Camus' theory of the great replacement, this is what white gay men share with the fate of the white race as a whole: both groups will be wiped off the face of the planet by a different and more potent race. Gay men are the canary in the racial coal mine, as it were: they will be the first to be overwhelmed. Not all white gay men are racial separatists. But the sinister logic Camus advances suggests that gay men and white people share a fear of being made extinct by the same threat. And his solution of 'replacement' suggests that your way of life can only ever be truly safe, your identity can only sustain itself as such at all when you control the means by which life – your life – is reproduced.

These fears aren't only projected onto the sweeping scales of global migration. They also manifest in something as intimate and private as gay men's thoughts and conversations about having children. In few books are these anxieties more painfully exposed than in Patrick Flanery's

The Ginger Child (2019), a memoir about Flannery and his husband's failed attempt to adopt a child in Britain. Flannery knows that adopting a child into a married gay couple is not the only way to raise a family; he knows 'performance artists and writers and queer scholars and activists' who have alternative family structures, and he is at pains to reassure us that his is a 'radically queer couple' who reject heteronormative relationship models and who refuse to self-identify to adoption services as something as simple as 'gay'. What makes this memoir so brutally honest is that Flannery knows all this and yet still admits he wants 'a child of my own'. He owns the 'selfishness of these desires', their contradictions with his professed politics, and his inability to escape them even when he knows they are the unwanted inheritance of his own upbringing by a heterosexual family. Few books more clearly show the psychic wounds and contradictions inflicted upon gay men by the urge to reproduce along the model of the heterosexual biological family: 'the desire, problematic as I know it is, for us to turn ourselves into that camera-ready middle-class same-sex couple with a toddling baby crawling across the lawn we don't have in front of the house we don't own.' This need for a child of his own, Flannery concludes, is 'hardwired, biological, even for a man like me'.

There is much that is compelling in this memoir: the account of the homophobia inflicted by adoption services on a gay couple, the honesty with which Flannery admits that he could not raise a child with a mental disability or with HIV. But what makes this memoir more than a record of one couple's experience of adoption is Flannery's reflection upon the envy produced when gay men desire to have children of 'their own'; that is, to have children the way a heterosexual couple have children. Flannery feels 'envious of pregnant women . . . envious of trans men who are able to become pregnant and give birth and then, miraculously, carry on being men . . . envious of people I know or meet with biological children who are smart, funny, well-adjusted . . . envious of that security and stability, that sense of uninterrogated connection'. Scrutinising himself, Flannery realises that envy, like desire, is a feeling produced by a lack: women, able to reproduce children, have something he does not. But that lack, he argues, is caused not by something missing in him but by a social inequality, the 'inequality of the ways in which reproduction is unevenly distributed'. This envy is a source of solidarity with women since they, too, reproduce in a world where the resources needed to give birth are unfairly shared: how many women can say they have total control over the conditions in which they choose or choose not to have children? This envy can be channelled into a motivation to build a world where the capacity to reproduce is shared more equitably – or, at least, to start the work of imagining what that world would look like. And yet, this sense of solidarity cannot be separated from the envy and lack that caused it in the first place. Even if we could create a more equitable system of collective reproduction, and a gay man like Flannery were to receive the children he yearns for from a willing surrogate, he would still 'never be able to be a (biological) mother to those children', but rather, as he puts it, 'in enacting my own parenthood, I will always envy the woman who carried that child or those children'. Contained in this conclusion is the assumption that women simply 'carry' children, that this gives them an unquestionable connection with that which they carry, that this never occurs in situations of precarity and danger or that carrying a child is always wanted. Flannery's memoir teaches us another way in which envy is like desire: what it seeks is a fantasy.

This envy is the consequence of giving up the fantasy of a gay planet: refusing to imagine a world where gay men can reproduce without women, whether by eliminating them altogether or stealing their eggs, renting their wombs and technologically replicating their bodies. If this is the price of a gay planet, it isn't one worth paying. The honesty of Flannery's memoir lies in his admission that this refusal has costs as well as compensations. Just like a pearl can only form around a speck of dirt, so too the solidarity gay men can feel towards women can only form around the recognition that, without a planet of their own, gay men need them in order to reproduce.

This mixture of envy and solidarity also drives a more public form in which gay men project their troubling fantasies and desires onto and about straight women: drag. In *How To Be Gay* (2014), a book that tries to salvage the impetus towards gay separatism by redefining gayness not as a sexual orientation but rather as an aesthetic, David M. Halperin goes so far as to say that the envy expressed by drag, at least in its traditional form, defines gayness as a style. Halperin gives the example of the Fire Island Widows, Italian American gay men who annually drag up as grieving Sicilian widows to mourn their friends and lovers who died of AIDS. Far from mocking grieving women, he argues that this act 'does not express hatred for women, so much as envy of some women's ability to carry off a public spectacle of private pain'. Undoubtedly constrained as women are in a patriarchal world, rituals do exist for their emotional suffering to be expressed. This is one thing that drag as an aesthetic act expresses: envy of the permission of public displays of emotion and suffering.

At the same time, men in drag accentuate the stereotypes of femininity to show just how limited this license is. Women can express emotion in public on the condition of playing roles: the grieving widow, the fierce Black bitch, the Essex hun. Drag doesn't express misogyny; it makes the stereotypes of misogyny public and makes them an object of serious humour. Drag of any kind begins to fail if the audience doesn't believe they are seeing a performance or if the performer stops thinking they are giving one. This is the basis of drag's claims to be subversive, to not simply replicate that which it mimics: only straights believe their gender is natural. The drag queen wants their audience to know that when the wigs come off, he returns to the very different advantages and disadvantages granted to gay men. But virtuous as this may sound, drag in this traditional form is an art that can only exist in a world that assumes a fundamental difference in kind between men and women. That's one reason why *RuPaul's Drag Race* for a long time refused, to intense controversy, to let trans women compete in his television show: as RuPaul claimed, 'drag loses its sense of danger and its sense of irony once it's not men doing it'. Of course, outside the limited parameters of a show clipped and plucked for mainstream consumption, drag flourishes in basement clubs in south London and Nairobi and Beijing in ever more polymorphous forms, fully welcoming to trans women and bioqueens – cisgendered queens assigned female at birth – even if the name bioqueens make them sound like aliens from a distant galaxy. But maybe that's because they are. RuPaul eventually let bioqueens into his version of drag, but his initial fear that drag would become meaningless is a fear that gay men as a distinct group would become extinct if we moved beyond a biological understanding of sex and the division of reproductive labour it presumes: women reproduce, gay men don't. If, for Ethan on Athos, the choice faced by gays for survival was 'race war or genocide', for RuPaul, it is gender difference or dragocide: all or nothing.

This is why the fear of extinction, which is nothing more than the fear of being forgotten, accompanies all these attempts to isolate and reproduce a distinctly gay world, whether that is the planet Athos, a gay Israel or a middle-class family of one's own. The desire to have one's own identity slides into the belief that only a separate planet can keep that identity safe. But this gay planet can only be produced and reproduced by relying upon women, who end up becoming the impossible-to-eradicate bad conscience of the dream of the gay planet. Or maybe the good conscience, because there does seem to be some block that has prevented gay men from fully elaborating a planet where they can reproduce themselves without women. There is some deep-seated fear of a gay planet, some subconscious acknowledgement that the kind of life it would preserve is not worth preserving. That might mean that deep in the gay unconscious, the love of femininity trumps the love of family. Or it might be evidence of a buried recognition that the reason the desire for gay reproduction without women is shadowed by the fear of extinction is because the dream of a gay planet, like all kinds of separatism, is a kind of death wish.

This death wish has produced the planet Mytra. Mytra is a planet that was colonised by a group of gay scientists fleeing persecution on Earth. They used cloning technology to ensure their planet's population only consists of men, but they never discovered a way to ensure all these men are gay since neither gayness nor same-sex desire can be genetically engineered. And so, all men are accompanied by robots to monitor any hints of heterosexuality, and all boys are systematically sexually abused to accustom them to same-sex intercourse. We know about Mytra from the adventures of a team of Christian missionaries who travel the galaxy saving lost souls. One missionary, Sarah, helps a Mytrian man to see the combined lights of Christianity and heterosexuality, converting him by lengthy theological sermons. Mytra appears in *The Disciplining of Mytra* (2009) by Rich Coffey, an American evangelical writer of Christian science fiction, as an imagined inspiration for missionary zeal. It is one of the rarest gay planets, one with a complete explanation of how gay men reproduce themselves: not just as men but as men with same-sex desire. And it was imagined in order to inspire its elimination: to ensure all gay men are in one place and then convert them out of existence. If the desire for the extinction of gay men drives successful fantasies of a gay planet, then fear of extinction causes the failed ones.

* * *

In the introduction to one of the earliest collections of queer theory, *Fear of a Queer Planet* (1993), Michael Warner describes the picture of a nude man and woman inscribed on *Pioneer*

10, the first man-made object to leave the solar system, as a reminder that 'speeds to the ends of the universe, announcing to passing stars that earth is not, regardless of what anyone says, a queer planet'. Academic queer theory since has been torn between two impulses towards building that planet. On the one hand, thinkers like Lee Edelman have argued that all political movements committed to a better future rely upon the fantasy of transmitting that future to 'the Child'. Our collective social 'future' is inherently a product of the very kind of biological reproduction that queerness should refuse. On the other, theorists like José Esteban Muñoz have argued that the alternative kinds of sociability and sexual connection created under the umbrella of queerness are glimmers of a utopian remaking of the world. We get closer to the queer planet with every anonymous hook-up in a cruising ground, with an act of labour that sustains a kinship network in place of the families we are born into. Yet, in imagining what aliens would think if all they knew about humanity were the drawings on the *Pioneer 10*, Warner is imagining a future in which queerness, and all its gloriously endless disagreements, would be forgotten. This seems to be one fear lurking beneath all these fantasies about planets and DNA, separatism, and surrogacy. Not just how can I reproduce, but how will I be remembered? And perhaps this fear is so strong that it has stunted the queer imagination. As if biological reproduction is the only way to ensure the remembrance of our current forms of life. As if our current forms of life and reproduction are the only way things could be.

In recent years, however, books like Maggie Nelson's *The Argonauts* (2015) and Sophie Lewis's *Full Surrogacy*

Now (2019) have posited queer forms of reproduction as the key to freeing us from the oppressions of capitalism and patriarchy and taking us closer to the queer utopia. This in turn produces the discomfiting effect that these oppressions become a task for queer thought – or even queer lives – to solve. Queerness is burdened with experimenting with the most radical forms of reproduction in order to solve the problems of capitalism for everyone else unhappy with the ways in which social and biological reproduction are currently woven together. Sometimes, these books rely upon the kind of technological determinism already evident in feminist speculations like Shulamith Firestone's *The Dialectic of Sex* (1970). In *Full Surrogacy Now*, Lewis exhorts us to imagine possibilities offered by reproductive technology that will decouple the social category of 'woman' from the act of gestation. But for decades, these possibilities have been imagined in the form of the gay planet, and the result of these technologies has not been to liberate women but to eradicate them. Yet, at other times, these books show the universalising ambitions of queerness at their best: straight people are right to fear a queer planet because a whole new world is exactly what queers want. Queers want to change everything: to create a world without patriarchy, capitalism, racism and environmental destruction. The happiness Nelson achieves in *The Argonauts* is the happiness of having it all: bearing her own child *and* being queer *and* being able to desire masculinity *and* not having to desire patriarchy *and* having a partner so understanding they will write in your book affirming your own writing. Hers was a queer pregnancy, she explains, because it showed someone 'wanting something both ways – and getting it'.

But what if this world doesn't yet offer what you want? What if one way towards creating a world that can give what you want is never to forget those that don't and to pass on, in stories, in memories, the fantasies, no matter how dark, that the limitations of those worlds produce? Whatever new galaxy is formed out of the remnants of our own, a gay planet won't be part of it, at least if the kind of gay men who discovered the reasons to be afraid of a gay planet have any say. And maybe they won't. Maybe gay men won't be part of that new galaxy either. What we call gay is just a temporary knot produced out of the tangle of how we presently understand bodies – 'male' – and desire – 'attracted only to men'. There was a time when the concept of gayness didn't exist, then it did, and maybe its time is already passing. After all, who would identify as gay – gym! shopping! masc-4-masc! – when you could be queer – politics! theory! fluidity! But gay also names a position in relation to the system of biological reproduction, a position in which your desire excludes that which reproduces your way of life. Gay desire depends on the very thing it excludes – women – in order to continue existing in the world.

If gay as an identity might not make it to the queer galaxy, there might be some value in maintaining, or at least not forgetting, gay as a position in relation to reproduction. There is something valuable in remembering that desire, in all the ways it might flow, doesn't have to be the desire to reproduce. There is something valuable, too, in accepting that to fulfil your desire to reproduce is to become dependent upon someone and something over which you have no claim or control and never will. The desire for a gay planet comes from the fear of being forgotten. It is our need to be remembered, in the end, that determines our desires. But if we change how we are remembered, if we look down from the stars and walk away from the family – who knows what might happen to what we want.

DUNGENESS

I was the only one in the carriage as the train left St Pancras. It was a bright Friday morning in May 2020. Before the doors closed, a man lazily wiped the handrails with a tea towel. He wasn't wearing a face mask. As the train pulled out of the station, I saw a sign I had never seen before: *St Pancras Cruising Club.* I made a note to join when I got back. Stratford International, Ebbsfleet International, Ashford International, stations that promised a now almost impossible escape from this island. At Ashford, change for Rye, from Rye, a cycle to Dungeness. With hands covered in latex gloves and disinfectant gel as if I was travelling to visit a patient in hospital, a patient to whom I was a threat, I stuffed the flakes of a croissant under the mask over my mouth. It had been months since I last ate a croissant, and I had forgotten what they tasted like. I had forgotten that they never taste right in England.

After Stratford, the train glides across marshlands and between motorways, pylons and graveyards of abandoned red buses. At the Dartford Crossing, it passes the Queen Elizabeth II Suspension Bridge, the only crossing of the Thames east of London. Every time I've taken this train, the bridge has appeared weighed down with trucks and lorries carrying the containers that, when offloaded, fill the yards along the river in expanding grids of rectangular colour. These yards were once the site of the docks themselves before they automated and decamped, like their former workers, to the coasts of Essex and Suffolk, both equally without sentiment. One way or another, everything has to get onto an island, and everyone has to get ahead in this world. Then the train suddenly plunges underground, passing beneath the miles and miles of warehouses that filter the goods in those shipping containers out into the homes and businesses of the city. The tunnel goes deep in order not to disturb the perfect flatness that robots require to move across warehouse floors. A variation as small as two millimetres can threaten to disrupt their automatic movement and our ceaseless consumption. These warehouses have become so large that, further out in the countryside, they are painted shades of blue so as to blend into the sky. It is an illusion worthy of Capability Brown, whose 18th-century gardens took landscapes long reshaped by human agriculture and transformed them back into wilderness, disguising with the appearance of nature the very source of those landowners' wealth.

High-tech bridges cloaked in the trappings of monarchy, industrial heritage either rusting in nostalgia or ruthlessly redeveloped, country homes disguising the extraction, human and agricultural, that paid for them. An illusion: this is what the English landscape had always been to me, which is why the English themselves have always been so hard for me to understand. They too seemed to only present me with surface appearances or to use an imagined past to disguise who they really were. By that summer, I had lived in England for ten years, and it had never felt like home. With the borders closed, if only temporarily, I had to imagine what it would be like to never leave, to face up to the fact that I had decided that this was where I was going to make my home. For there were reasons I had decided to live in England, people I wanted to live with, people who didn't exist in the home that was given to me. That summer I was travelling to visit one of them again.

The train emerges into a gash cut through the earth; the concrete walls left rough as if the engineers had run out of money. On this trip to Dungeness, my third, the trees outside London looked like they were presenting the colours of their foliage for the very first time. Small delicate leaves of translucent pale greens and tender nervous yellows. Colours that could only appear because the trees had been spared their regular spring pollution. A quarry revealed the first sight of the chalk that stretches from Essex right down to the cliffs of Dover, the entrance this country opens to the world: sparkling, uniform, white.

Approaching Rye, the trees disappear, and green fields become crisscrossed with canals and daubed with white sheep. Rows of pylons draw parallel lines of wires all the way to a looming box on the horizon, mauve against the bright cornflour sky. To one side of the cycle path between Rye and Dungeness, along a barbed-wire fence that separated the path from the dunes that open onto the sea, a parade of giant red flags marched in single file. As I cycled past, I heard what first sounded like delicate firecrackers and then like an axe striking a tree. In a Ministry of Defence Firing Range, soldiers were shooting, perfecting the art of killing.

Dungeness is a spit of land jutting out into the English Channel. It is a plain of sand and shingle, flat and low in all directions, with no fences or walls. Along with Cape Canaveral in Florida, it is the largest formation of shingle on the surface of the earth. It receives the most sunlight and least rainfall of anywhere in England. The landscape is pockmarked with old wooden cottages and new artists' studios and littered with abandoned ships, empty oil tanks, shipping containers and half-finished breezeblock huts. Looming over everything are two lighthouses, black and white, and a nuclear power station that sends lines of pylons and wires inland away from the sea. Fishermen come from all around the surrounding towns and villages to fish in what they call 'the boil', the currents heated by the hot wastewater expelled by the reactor, whose high temperatures attract the smaller sea creatures upon which fish come to feed. The fish get trapped in the currents, and some are killed when they get sucked into the reactor's cooling system, providing easy prey for the flocks of seagulls who circle overhead. Dungeness is the end of England, and it feels like the end of the world.

Dungeness is home to Prospect Cottage, two small single-story buildings made of caulked black wood with lemon yellow windowpanes, a triangular roof of corrugated iron and a chimney with two orange terracotta flues. On the front, two large windows frame a narrow door. On the gable end to the right, a staircase rises to a small yellow door opening into an attic. On the left, the text of John Donne's 'The

Sunne Rising' is mounted in carved black wooden letters, dismissing the claims of the sun it faces: 'Love, all alike, no season knows nor clime / Nor hours, days, months, which are the rags of time.' The back of the main building slopes down to a kitchen with a long horizontal window, divided into squares. A second smaller cottage added onto the right forms half a courtyard at the back. Inside it now is a kind of sunroom stuffed with soft-chairs, browning cacti and a Jesus hanging on a crucifix. From 1987 until his death in 1994, Prospect Cottage was where Derek Jarman came almost weekly to escape the demands of producing his films and the treatments for the illnesses that slowly consumed him. As the sun set each day behind the three nuclear reactors looming over the rear of the cottage, it was where he came to find the time to read, write and be alone.

Jarman was a filmmaker, a poet, a painter and, for many, a saint. That was the myth others imposed upon him by virtue of a life of activism that often simply took the form of being himself in public without shame. Every artist creates their own myth, an origin story about why they have to make the work they do. Otherwise, creation becomes, if not impossible, then haunted with bad conscience. Why am I making this? Greed, a need for attention, the lust for money, the mere chance of the day. Jarman, who believed so much in the power of myths that he spent much of his life attacking those that warp our desire, presents his origin story in his journals published as *Dancing Ledge* (1984), *Modern Nature* (1991) and *Smiling in Slow Motion* (2000), and his collective history of British gay life, *At Your Own Risk* (1992). He was born in 1942, the child of a fading Empire, of a New Zealand father recruited into the RAF and an

English mother whose father was a tea trader in Calcutta. After decades of repression and an art school education in London, he joined the waves of queer people emerging into public in a riot of pleasure throughout the sixties and seventies, living in warehouses and cruising on piers and joyfully threatening patriarchy, heterosexuality and the family with films like *Sebastiane* (1976), his first full-length feature – a homoerotic life of Saint Sebastian, the dialogue completely in Latin – which contains, or so Jarman claimed, one of the first erections shown on a film approved by the British Film Classification Board. But just as in the myth of Icarus, whose wings melted by flying too close to the sun, the dream of sexual liberation fell back to earth with the election of Margaret Thatcher and the arrival of HIV. Jarman became one of the first prominent British people to announce they were HIV positive in 1987 and demonstrated by publishing books, producing films and exhibiting paintings that this was no barrier to the richest of lives. Thus was born the legend of Saint Derek who, in choosing to use his life to raise awareness of the spread of HIV and what it meant to live with AIDS (including what it meant to continue to have sex with AIDS), saved the lives of thousands of people.

Jarman spent more and more of his time in Dungeness from 1987 onwards, planting his garden, writing his diaries. His body weakened, his eyesight failed, his memories bloomed. Now tourists come to Prospect Cottage from around the world, and a few months before my visit, a fundraiser secured enough money to preserve the cottage and its garden as a memorial to his life. His death had become a work of art, as had happened with his beloved Saint Sebastian, suggesting that such a transfiguration may have been what Jarman had wanted, perverting the rituals of Christianity even beyond the grave.

Like the tourists, I too had become a worshipper of Saint Derek. My prayers began when I first saw the grainy beauty of *The Last of England* (1987), late at night on Channel 4, the source of so many illicit teenage pleasures in those years when the internet hadn't fully arrived in the rural Ireland where I grew up. Not just because of his art, his activism, his good looks and his transcendence of shame. But, above all, because of what he achieved with the Prospect Cottage garden. He had decided how he would be remembered. He had made his own memorial.

Yet the Prospect Cottage garden is, for me at least, more than just a memorial to Jarman's death. To reduce it to that gives his life a destination, a telos, a conclusion. The problem with this is not that his whole life becomes defined by the fact that he died of AIDS. This has become a tragic cliché imposed on the lives of a whole generation of gay artists, but to elide the reason for their deaths can itself become a cliché of disavowal. Rather the problem lies in the shape imposed on a life by the ending itself: a line that moves from beginning to end. This is a line we can only see once that end has taken place, which means it is a line none of us can ever see while living. This makes it the most unnatural of shapes to place on a life, or at least, no less unnatural than any of the shapes we can put on a life. The Prospect Cottage garden was one of Jarman's works of art, a story in itself, not the end to his life story. It has its own shapes, its own lines. It tells its own endings, its own beginnings.

* * *

The landscape of shingle in which Jarman planted his garden is no windswept desert devoid of living things. Its stones are home to thickets of sea kale with their spiky purple fringes, delicate blooms of sea campion the colour of dark red wine and flesh clumps of sebum, whose tips shade from green to pink. These plants share the shingle with the waste of an entire country. Plastic bags shining white in the sun, black rubber tires worn smooth by the wind, a purple blanket made of synthetic fur, settling in folds for centuries of slow, glistening degradation. Among the plants and litter, like way stations on a pilgrimage, are rusting fragments of mysterious machinery. Shipping chains lie coiled on the ground in perfect circles. A giant metal wheel with a serrated rim lies on its side, a brilliant rusting orange against the dun ochre of the shingle. A stilled engine, white and grey, extends an axle that no longer turns in search of a gear shaft that no longer exists. This tableau of frozen motion is mounted on a platform made of driftwood. Dungeness makes a spectacle out of the persistence of plastic and the ruins of industry.

The Prospect Cottage garden was formed by scavenging these scraps of civilisation and the plants and stones between them. In front of the house, flints planted upright into the shingle mark out flower beds: rectangles, squares and circles. At the back, plants nestle within raised beds made of driftwood planks and among the spherical weights that were once used to drag down fishing nets. When I visited in May, the beds teemed with purple foxgloves and pink opium poppies, with crimson valerian and indigo viper's bugloss, with white sea rose and pink peony, and between all this colour rose voluptuous clouds of curry plant, just on the cusp of blooming. Jarman began to lay out his garden the year he was diagnosed with HIV, which was the same year in which he met the love of his life, known in his diaries as HB, who eventually came to live with him at Prospect Cottage. For Jarman, the time of the gardener, the time of transience and cyclical returns, was as much about staying in the eternal present of love as it was a means to turn away from an impending future of death: 'The gardener digs in another time without past or future, beginning or end.' Each summer, the flowers return, the best reminder of the transient present of the gardening, and perhaps this is why Jarman also wrote that 'Dungeness is at its best in the golden light of summer'.

I preferred the garden in winter, when I visited it the year before, when all the plants were dead apart from the clumps of gorse that surrounded the cottage-like prickly fortified walls. In the astringent January sun, the garden's other unnatural plants could assert their presence. These, to me, were truer to the gardener who had planted them than the flowers and blossoms of summer. In front of the house, clusters of grey stones were formed out of oblong flints planted upright into the shingle. Smooth stones, with holes worn through them by the sea, were fixed on top of thin branches of wood, bleached white by sun and salt. They looked like the first totems created to sanctify reproduction, male wood piercing female stone. Yet here they were petrified and frozen amidst the act of copulation and had become nothing more than the prettiest of decorations.

In the back garden, rusting metal poles stood topped with hooks and coils amidst a freezing January wind. Chains with flaking links marked out circles and loops between empty beds of earth, the spaces in which wood

and metal had been bred into new hybrid species. Thick
logs of bleached wood bristled with clunky, primitive
iron nails. Tall driftwood planks were crowned with iron
triangles and coiled metal springs, evoking medieval
weaponry or crude chastity devices. Closer to the cottage,
new species were forming from the coupling of other
materials. A necklace of stones hung down from a small
wooden pole, strung along a loop of metal chain. A dead
branch pierced a round of cork and a hexagonal bolt. A
rusted spring coiled around a pointed stick that forced its
way through the hole of a stone. A wooden pole wore a
cork collar while being embraced by a metal spring. These
inorganic couplings and triplings oscillated between
looking like dead creatures and the organs that produced
them. They were simultaneously the symbols and reality
of their own monstrous gestation.

Jarman's cinematic tribute to his 'wilderness of failure',
The Garden (1990), opens with footage of these plants lit
up at night by massive banks of electric floodlights. The
film then goes on to sanctify Dungeness by making it the
backdrop for the story of a gay Jesus: his birth, his loves,
his death and his resurrection. It makes his garden a shrine,
but it can only do so by borrowing the aura of holiness from
the Christianity it claims to despise. The leather pig who
writhes among the shingle under the glare of the floodlights
in the film's opening scene needs Jesus more than anyone,
for it is those who require their pleasures to be a sin who are
most in need of a saviour. If Jarman's garden deserves to be
a site of worship, then what should be worshipped is what
is revealed under blinding electric lights as much as bleak
winter sun: that this is a wholly artificial paradise.

These winter plants are more faithful to the landscape from which they spring than the organic beauties of sea pea, peony or digitalis. Dungeness may be classified as a nature reserve, perhaps the only nature reserve that includes a nuclear fission reactor, but it is a place that shows up the illusion of its own classification. There is no longer any 'nature' that can be isolated from the impact of our species; there is nothing we haven't touched with our metal, our plastic, our litter. For some, this is a tragic fall from grace, a sin to be expiated by seeking out wild places or rewilding the places we have. But nothing is as artificial as 'wildness', nothing as inhumane as wanting to expunge others from the land so that you can enjoy a view. Dungeness is a reminder that this fall from nature is what makes us who we are. Or rather, that we shouldn't think of ourselves as living after a fall at all. We can't create reservations to preserve something called nature because we are always at once of and apart from the world, as much in our ageing bodies as with our shimmering synthetic fabrics. Simply because of what we are and what we do, we cannot be ruled by an appeal to what is natural. Jarman dug his garden in this landscape that dispels the illusion that there is anything natural about the world in which we live. His winter plants try to pass on memory in a world where this doesn't just naturally happen. Where we have to make it happen.

These winter plants are also more faithful, it seemed to me that second visit, to the life of the person who made them. In his films and in his life, Jarman waged a joyful war against all notions of what was natural when it came to sexuality and desire. His goal, however, was not to replace them with a newer and better nature but to rejoice in the creation of what we normally call artifice in order to dissolve the division between the natural and the artificial once and for all. Jarman knew that the cure promised by his garden was a chimaera, but he loved it all the same. 'I plant my herbal garden as a panacea, read up on all the aches and pains that plants will cure – and know they are not going to help. The garden as a pharmacopoeia has failed. Yet there is a thrill in watching the plants spring up that gives me hope.'

The garden at Prospect Cottage is an illusion: a panacea, a placebo. The plants do not grow from the shingle: how could they? They grow from clumps of manure filled into holes dug into the stones. And the solitude Jarman sought and experienced at Prospect Cottage was achieved by a similar kind of *trompe d'œil*, a painter's deception of the eye. Jarman's diaries record the weeks spent tending his garden at Dungeness, the days spent painting and writing alone, the hours spent in bed dealing with pain and sickness; but they also record almost constant motion back and forth to London, to hospitals and Pride demonstrations and nights cruising in Hampstead Heath and gallery openings and coffee in Soho, and they record the constant care he received from his companion HB. Dungeness, he knew, merely offered him the 'illusion of isolation', for isolation can only ever be an illusion. However, much we think we need to be alone, whether to paint, or write, or simply survive, the absence of others is simply a sleight of hand. We might not see them, but they are still taking care of us, perhaps no time more than when not being present. They gift us the presence of their absence. Anonymity, alienation, the fiction that is autobiography; so much is based on forgetting what it really means to be alone: that we could never be just ourselves, even if we wanted to.

Jarman knew his garden was no less of a conjuring trick than his films, those temporary apparitions of another world in light and colour. In the last book he wrote before he died, he offered a guide to his garden and the plants and flowers he grew there: 'I would like anyone who reads my book to try this wildness in a corner. It will bring you much happiness.' His garden preserves the memory of his deep need to be alone at times in order to be happy. But it is also a reminder that our experience of solitude, like Jarman's patch of wilderness in a corner of England, can only ever be a grand theatrical production, staged for an audience of one, by those set designers and choreographers that are our friends and lovers. It is a memorial to our need for the illusion of solitude. What enables us to bear the fact that we are always bound to others is the ability to experience their absence in our imagination, in fantasies that others let become our reality.

Jarman could live his mirage of solitude because, for all that Dungeness seems to be the end of the world, it is, in fact, less than two hours from London by train and taxi. On one of his trips down from London, Jarman records that his taxi driver 'made me very worried by his insistence on talking about radioactivity. He said nothing would persuade him to live at Dungeness, life was precious'. The taxi driver was not wrong. The plants in the Prospect Cottage garden bear traces of radioactivity emitted from the nuclear reactors. The sea kale is especially absorbent. Dungeness is a place that reminds us of another illusion, that of complete safety, and it is equally a testament to our need, one perhaps less conscious, to take risks in the pursuit of happiness. It is a challenge to live honestly with the risks that come with desire, for what could more signify someone willing to live with the consequences of risk, the threat that in seeking happiness you might cut yourself off from others, than someone who chose to live their final years in the shadow of a nuclear power plant?

The winter flowers of wood and stone, with their tendrils of rusted springs and coiled wire, purchase their persistence among the winds of Dungeness at the cost of eschewing the organic cycle of repetition and return, blooming and wilting, fertilisation and germination. In this, they stand as a memorial to a life that cannot haunt us. Ghosts are the shadows of natural life; they are the repetition of the natural cycle gone awry, continuing to return when they no longer should. When we allow ourselves to be haunted by the past – for it is always we who desire to be haunted – we impose upon the dead the expectation that they still should return, like a flower blooming each spring. That expectation can only be disappointed, so they return in images of nature gone wrong: rotten corpses, broken bodies, preternaturally young and stunted children. Jarman's artificial flowers allow him to be remembered without the disappointment that would turn him into a ghost; that is, without the expectation that he should be still alive, which is the expectation that he should have lived differently. Right until the end of his life, Jarman considered himself 'the luckiest film-maker of his generation', and it was essential to how he chose to die that he believed, and needed others to believe, that he wouldn't have lived any other kind of life. His garden deserves more than to be seen as a memorial of death, and it gives us something better than a past that haunts us.

A few days after this winter visit, I went to see Jarman's final film, *Blue* (1993), in the Prince Charles Cinema just off Leicester Square. *Blue* presents a single image: one continuous shot of luminous bright blue, the blue you find right above you in a clear winter sky, projected onto the screen for an hour and fifteen minutes. As the film opens, a voice announces: 'Blue flashes in my eyes.' This is the blue of an eye test taken after Jarman's sight began to fade in 1990 due to an onset of toxoplasmosis, lesions in the brain that cause parts of the body to shut down. 'My vision will never come back', the voice of this visual artist announces. 'I have to come to terms with sightlessness.' *Blue* is a film of loss, not just of sight, but of friends and lovers. 'I have no friends now who are not dead or dying.' The beach at Dungeness has become the place for the recital of their names. Over the sound of the sea, he recalls them: David, Howard, Graham, Paul, Derek, Terry . . . Yet, if blue is the colour of loss, it is also the colour of 'an infinite possibility becoming tangible'. *Blue* makes us face the loss of colour, but it also offers us the chance to 'fight the fear that engenders the beginning, the middle and the end. For in blue, there are no boundaries or solutions. Time is what keeps the light from reaching us.' Sitting in the cinema, we see nothing but light, we escape time, we get a glimpse of what it looks like to die.

Blue is Jarman's most stark and inhospitable film, and that is what makes it so beautiful. It allows you to do only one thing: to stare at the blue light, giving your eye no freedom to wander over the myriad details that slip into the background of other film shots. With no choice but to sit and stare and listen alone, you discover the possibilities that can come from seeing only one thing, as Jarman himself was discovering, as he slowly saw less and less as he lost his sight while making the film. You notice the texture of sounds, the presence of the absence that is silence. And you notice the strange sociability of cinema spectatorship, a communal unspoken agreement to be mutually inhospitable. The screen becomes a blue light that illuminates the strangers with whom you are sitting in the twilight for an hour or two, each one of you silent and not speaking, yet sharing the experience of seeing alone, together, which is the only way we can share the prospect of death.

In the freezing January sun, the holiday homes around Dungeness were empty. The fish and chips restaurants were closed, and the only place I could get something to eat before returning home was the pub at the furthest end of the peninsula, surrounded by empty caravans and overlooked by the lighthouses. Seeking shelter before the long journey home, I escaped from the freezing cold into the smell of beer, vinegar and hostility.

I first travelled to Dungeness in August 2017 during the second of the long hot summers that followed England's vote to leave to the European Union. As if the weather was trying to remind the country of the impossibility of its desire to disconnect from the continent, the heat that burned the grass in the parks of London was blamed on a so-called 'Spanish plume', a meteorological system funnelling hot air up from the Iberian Peninsula. Not that many were complaining, perhaps because 'Spanish plume' is a much cuter term than anthropogenic climate heating. That year, the trains that left

London for the seaside were full all summer long, families packing themselves onto another link to the European continent, the high-speed train to Dover, to speed as fast as they could on borrowed technology to Margate, Broadstairs, Botany Bay, Camber Sands and on to Dungeness.

On the train to Ashford, red poppies were stuck to the corner of each window. A father in a kippah warned two boys that the temperature was going to be over 30 degrees Celsius, and he sounded like he was taking a strange pleasure in warning them they had to be very, very careful in that kind of heat. A girl beside me shaped purple clay into a ball and smeared it against the back of the hot plastic seat. She peeled it off, rolled it into a ball and smeared it against the seat again. A Welsh man's voice complained that there was a shortage of storage units all around Swansea. I ate my travel snacks: fresh figs and dried dates. Two train guards stood at the door, waiting to change shifts at Ashford. 'I like this job, believe it or not.' 'It's not a lot, is it?' 'It's not.' 'It's the diversity.' 'I like how I can get up a civilised time.' 'I get up at quarter to seven; I have time to do everything I need.' 'I get up a six-fifteen, so I have time to wash the wig, otherwise it sticks right up.' 'I like it. I do.'

The smaller train from Ashford to Rye was so full of bicycles and prams that there was no room for passengers to join at the smaller village stations of Ham Street and Appledore. An older woman, sitting on the folded seat by the door, announced the disappointing news at both stops. 'There are no seats left. There is no room. You're not getting on lovely and especially not with that buggy.' Like all true performers, she knew how to pause for effect. She waited until we had left the cursing mothers and crying children at the platform to announce: 'There's just too many people here, isn't there? There is barely even room for me.' They say that those moments when everyone in a room goes quiet at the same time are proof that feelings can be collective, not just individual. 'I live here, and there is hardly even a seat for me. Two carriages and barely even a seat for me. There is just no room for me.'

As the crowd waited for the bus that went from Rye to Camber Sands beach and then onto Dungeness, a girl announced that someone in Eastbourne had posted a picture of the sea. 'You can't see a thing.' 'It's like it's all cloud'. The problem was not the English weather. A girl announced that a chemical haze had drifted in from the continent and was poisoning people. A woman in Beachy Head had gone into toxic shock. People in Birling Gap were saying their eyes were burning and that they couldn't breathe. An old woman was airlifted to hospital. A few minutes later, a woman saw online that Sussex police had ordered all beaches in the vicinity to be evacuated. But her boyfriend pointed out that it only covered the East Sussex coast. 'We're fine.' So people put away their phones when the bus arrived and crowded on regardless.

Shot on Jarman's trademark Super-8 film, *The Last of England* opens with footage of young men demolishing factories before sitting down to shoot heroin and masturbate over a reproduction of Caravaggio's *Amor Vincit Omnia* (1602), a painting of Cupid in the form of a young boy offering his naked body to the viewer. Home videos of a technicolour 1950s childhood are cut with footage of riots and burning cities: footage of Imperial pomp in India alternates with drive-through shots of endless boarded up council homes in Liverpool. As clear as this narrative of historical decline may be, the film has little in the way of plot or script, bar a voice intoning over footage of Jarman at his desk that compares the damaged young men who flit across the film's industrial wasteland to the poppies cut down in Flanders Fields, the English soldiers who died in the First World War. This is a film that thinks in images: the barrel of a gun, a shining leather boot, the embers that keep a group of refugees warm. And it is a film with a strange relationship to its images. The camera is in constant motion, jerking and shaking as it circles a boy being executed by firing line or as it loops around a frenzied Tilda Swinton who is trying to tear herself out of a white wedding dress as the world burns down behind her. Above all, it is a film of fire: orange bonfires, burning buildings and blinding phosphorescent flares.

Months later, reading his diaries, I would learn that in Jarman's alchemical cosmology, fire could be purifying and transforming, as it was in *Jubilee* (1978), the next film I sought out. *Jubilee* begins with Queen Elizabeth I being offered a vision of the future of her kingdom by the Elizabethan magician John Dee, a figure with whom Jarman long identified. That vision turns out to be one of a group of punks living in a squat in the London docklands, led by the magnetic Jordan as Amyl Nitrate and Toyah Wilcox as Madd. *Jubilee* is a deeply cynical film, presenting the punk aesthetic it exploits as nothing more than a fabrication of media corporations. It ends with the cast of squatters selling out and moving to living in a country house with the corporate baron Borgia Ginz, who gleefully concludes: 'They all sign up one way or another.' It is also one that sees some possibility of renewal in its destruction, the possibility of a renewal for England. Amyl Nitrate is 'England's glory', and she rewrites England's history as one of a ruinous self-oppression by its own worst tendencies. The angel conjured up by John Dee to present Elizabeth with this vision of her realm exhorts her to 'consider the world's diversity and worship it'. This is the sense of renewal through destruction that, ten years later, is absent in *The Last of England*, perhaps because most of those punks really did sell out and move into country houses. Yet, what gives that film its strange charge is a lingering ambivalence about the England that has destroyed itself. In one sequence, two men, one naked, one in military uniform, both drunk, wrestle and then fuck on top of a massive Union Jack flag. It wasn't clear to me then, and it's still not clear to me now, whether that flag is being desecrated or sanctified anew. And nor has it ever been clear to me, then or now, how this celebration of queer transgression could also be a lament for the betrayal of England.

The bus to Dungeness passes through the village of Lydd, whose medieval church was the tallest building for miles around until the nuclear power station was built in 1965. It was so hot on that first trip that I got out at Lydd and walked along a long straight road past the fence that marked out the perimeter of the power plant and then past the caravans and holiday homes that fill the shingle as you approach the shore. I passed a painted placard fixed to a wire fence: 'STOLEN: Dirty thieves for the third time broke in and stole my electric fence unit and two batteries, etc. I have the unit, come on, please.' Another sign was stuck outside a mobile home: 'Next Door Stop Looking Into My Bedroom Window.'

I wanted a long walk past the sea, so instead of immediately heading south down to the peninsula to Prospect Cottage, I turned north to loop past down the shoreline. On the way, I passed a quarry and, on the tarmac path outside, a long chalk message had been scrawled under the baking August sun. 'Basically, I have cheated on my boyfriend and haven't told him. I feel so bad about it. But I realised that I did it because I'm bored because he never sees me anymore and I waited six months for him to want to be with me. I am bored of being with someone who isn't with me all the time when I personally love being around other people. Because I am a very sociable person. I am going to tell him. But it will hurt him so much. He tells me off a lot and gets annoyed when I spend time with other people and when I smoke even though he got expelled for drugs and substances. I am also attracted to other people, which suggests to me that I don't only have eyes for him which isn't fair on him. Anyways, Penelope.'

Jarman's concern with England runs throughout all his films, surfacing more clearly in some more than others. The next film he made after the *Last of England* was *War Requiem* (1989), where to the soundtrack of Benjamin Britten's music and choral setting of the same name and Wilfred Owen's war poetry, Jarman composed a visual story of a veteran remembering his time in the trenches of the First World War. It is hard, at first, to see what unites the turn towards the sounds and images of the most sentimental kind of Englishness with the shattering of nationalist pieties that energises *Jubilee* and *The Last of England*. Or with Jarman's claim to have spent his life in a constant battle against what he called 'Heterosoc', the entire social system propped up by making heterosexuality the imaginative norm: capitalism, imperialism, war, the whole rotten lot. Taken as a lament for 'the truth untold, the pity of war', where the story of the suffering of an unknown English soldier is interspersed with a montage of footage of war from across the 20th century, the films anti-war message makes a certain kind of sense. Compulsory heterosexuality is not just violent, it is violence, an act of domination and source of pain right to its very core. And so too does the historical parallel the film implicitly draws between one entire generation of young men extinguished by the indifference of generals sending them to die in the trenches, killed by the indifference of the government, to the lives of gay men as HIV spread throughout the 1980s. But to focus a lament on the pity of war on the death of a beautiful young man is to fuel the nationalism that is part and parcel of 'Heterosoc', the kind of nationalism that measures its strength against the young man as a measure of male virility. When, in *War Requiem*, an officer cries over the body of a young infantryman while the German soldier who killed him lies dead in the snow behind them or when that German soldier reappears to lay a wreath of poppies at the feet of that infantryman, now resurrected as Saint George holding his red and white crossed flag, one wonders whether the problem with war is that it kills, or whether it kills Englishmen.

As in *Edward II* (1991), Jarman sought to weave queer desire into the history of English power, not to destroy that power. This film adapts Christopher Marlowe's 1592 play of the same name, making explicit the subtext widely believed, then and now, that Edward II had a sexual relationship with his courtier Piers Gaveston. In order to rewrite history for his present or write it properly for the first time, the film mixes contemporary and historical costuming and props, as in Jarman's previous film, *Caravaggio* (1986), which similarly attempted to bring to the surface the same-sex desire of a historical figure. Yet, if *Caravaggio* is a stilted museum piece, *Edward II* brings past and present into a time-bending collision, as when Jarman cast his fellow queer activists of the early 1990s as Edward's rebel army, supporting the king with their signs: 'Silence = Death', 'Gay Desire is Not a Crime'. These films betray an erotic fascination with male power and male suffering, with men who have the power to inflict suffering and men who have the power to endure it. The soldier dying in the trenches is an unemployed factory worker and is Saint Sebastian bleeding on the stake. The figure of the king and the imagined community of the nation is a means of amplifying the intensity of that power and suffering to extend the bounds of that power's reach and to bind those suffering into a brotherhood of men. That is why Englishness is inextricable from Jarman's vision of queer sexuality and why his sexuality was inextricable from his Englishness. Chains and nails like beneath the peony and daffodils of Dungeness.

Jarman's queerness is not just English. It is used to desire England: its innocence, its stoicism, its gardens and, above all, its beautiful young men. It only cares for women when they tend to these men, as with the nurse in *War Requiem* or when they take the form of queens for them to worship: Amyl Nitrate in *Jubilee*, Tilda Swinton as a post-industrial Britannia. This came from his love of illusions, and this was what taught me that England is the most illusory of places. The leisure of country estates was built on the labour of slaves; immaterial wealth is conjured into existence behind the stone pillars of the Bank of England; a vicious sense of superiority hides behind the politest of smiles; all the languages of the world flourish behind a façade of received pronunciation. Maybe Jarman's saving grace is that he knows these illusions are illusions, that he is like Prospero in his film adaptation of Shakespeare's *The Tempest* (1979), who knows when to put down his wand and accept 'our revels now have ended'. But maybe he is more like Shakespeare's contemporary, the alchemist and magician John Dee; maybe he truly believed he could turn base metal into gold, maybe he truly forgot the emptiness behind his illusions of England.

There are a lot of things I like about England. I like the Tube, I like Alison Moyet, I like Manchester drag queens (all of them, without exception), I like Camberwell Green and Burgess Park, I like the suya spots on the Old Kent Road, I like the coleslaw at Nando's, I like 'Flowers' by Sweet Female Attitude, and I like 'Making Plans for Nigel' by XTC. I like *The Continuous Katherine Mortenhoe* (1973) by D. G. Compton, and I like Jane Austen (who, contrary to popular wisdom, didn't like England at all). I like John Akomfrah and Shelagh Delaney, I like the Free Cinema Movement, and I like Yorkshire rhubarb.

And there are a lot of things about England I don't like. I don't like country houses, I don't like the Mitfords, I don't like (whisper it) Virginia Woolf, I don't like cricket (though I also don't understand it), I don't like the royal family (they should be abolished), I don't like the Proms, I don't like a privatised postal service, I don't like Yarl's Wood Immigration Removal Centre, I don't like that there is a gap in the National Archives where records of the torture of the

Mau Mau should be, and I don't like that anyone in England has been forced to use a food bank, even once.

But I'm here, and so is everyone else, each with their idiosyncratic likes and dislikes. So, what then? Part of what has made England feel like it has been slowly collapsing since I moved here in 2010 is that the people who live here can't even find a way to ask the question: how do we want to live together? The luxury of finding that question boring is a bit like that afforded by those views of fake wilderness on 18th-century country estates. It is the luxury of not even having to see those people upon whom you depend, for by living anywhere, you depend upon others. It is not at all like the fear that prevents one from asking that question because, having asked it once before, you were answered in no uncertain terms that you belong only so long as you remain silent and invisible.

England was never a nation-state in the classic sense (although, what was?). It was the centre of an Empire, where people living in England chose a government that ruled people living elsewhere who had no say in that government. By any metric, that means the English weren't participating in a democracy until about the 1960s, so maybe the problem is that living together democratically is just new to us all. By the time the Empire collapsed, and Britain joined the European Community, it had brought people to England who never could and never had to feel English and who sought solace in a Great Britain, or a United Kingdom, right at the moment when it began to devolve itself out of existence. English nationalists are right that immigration and the European Union mean the end of England; they are just wrong to believe their England ever existed. England can't be a nation-state like most other places – though it is not unique and a belief in exceptionalism is the true *vice anglais*. People in England need to find a way of being together that breaks the spell of old illusions and remains aware of the artifice of the new ones they will have to agree to have in common. It needs a way of being together where people can be alone in their idiosyncrasies. I often wonder if England needs to become more like Dungeness.

'God, the English are a queer bunch', announces the boy in *Wittgenstein* (1993), Jarman's penultimate feature-length film. *Wittgenstein* is a biopic, of sorts, charting the philosopher's lifelong attempt at 'trying to define for us limits of language, and what it is to have communication, one with another', a journey that saw him shift from viewing language as a picture of the world towards seeing it as the expression of a form of life. This was his discovery, as he tells his lover Johnny in bed, played by Jarman's own companion, HB, that: 'There is no private meaning. We are what we are because we share a common language and common forms of life.' Two images of solitude bookend the film. Near the beginning, the boy Wittgenstein sits at a sewing machine, surrounded by a cacophonous circle of adults reading books at him until he can no longer stand it and covers his ears and closes his eyes. 'I was to spend a lifetime disentangling myself from my education', he tells us. To the extent that Wittgenstein has a lesson for the English, this is it: if they are ever going to be able to live with one another, they will first have to undertake a lifetime of unlearning. They will have to dispel themselves of their illusions. They will have to remember their past for the very first time, so they can tell it to others so they can decide whether to make England their home. The second is an image of an adult Wittgenstein in a giant birdcage, sitting with a bird in a smaller cage, reflecting on the contradiction between trying to live a philosophy where meaning is simply the common use of language in public and living in a world where the public expression of his homosexuality is impossible. Wittgenstein tells us that he wanted to move philosophy away from being a picture of the 'lonely human soul, brooding over its private experiences . . . locked out from contact with others by the walls of their bodies'. But he could only do so, the end of the film reveals, by moving to Ireland to live alone in a cottage by the sea. In order to learn how to speak to others, he had to first be alone.

The English aren't half as queer as Jarman would have liked to think. In the end, he never dispelled himself of the illusions of Englishness. England was where he wanted to find a home: among gay kings, queer soldiers and punk queens. We all need illusions in which to feel at home. England was his. But his England wouldn't be mine. England, Jarman taught me, perhaps despite himself, has always been a kind of illusion. In the landscape over which it fell, I could live my own illusion. I didn't need to copy his.

In 1991, the Sisters of Perpetual Indulgence, a sisterhood of gay men who dress as nuns and travel the world rewarding the efforts of activists, conducted a ceremony of beatification on the shingle of Dungeness, canonising Jarman into their queer pantheon. By that third trip, I had lost not just my illusions but also my faith. Jarman deserves better than to be made a saint. He deserves better than devotion since that isn't love but servitude. The bad kind of love for an artist can be seen as a kind of desire gone wrong by needing that which it loves to be exceptional in order to make the lover the exception. The good kind can be learned from the art of loving differently. 'Sexuality colours my politics,' Jarman wrote, 'I distrust all figures of authority, including the artist.' 'Homosexuals have such a struggle to define themselves against the order of things,' he explained, 'an equivocal process involving the desire to be both "inside" and "outside".' As a result, he concluded, 'I distrust those with blueprints for our salvation'. After that final third trip, I no longer needed Jarman's blueprint for my salvation. Nor his art, since that too deserves our distrust: 'Only when art is demoted to the ranks again, treated as nothing remarkable, will our culture start to breathe.' As do those, he taught me, who proclaim sexuality or desire a form of salvation. 'These names – gay, queer, homosexual – are limiting, I would love to be finished with them.' To always want to imagine being finished with everything that has made you what you are. That too is a kind of desire. A desire worth remembering.

FÉLIX AND CATHY

One Sunday morning in June 2020, I left home to cross London to seek out my fortune. Not wealth. Not money. Not the financial prosperity that has drawn people into and across this city for as long as it has existed but the older kind of fortune that was once believed to be its cause, and still is, much as we are taught to believe otherwise. On a perfectly sunny day, the sky only blue, I set off in search of some fortune cookies that were lying in piles around the city so that I could take one and see what message lay inside.

I went in search of these cookies to submit myself to fortune's paradoxical mix of chance and fate. A good fortune is both something that happens to us by chance, luck or through sheer random occurrence, and our fortune is also our fate, the script for our lives written in advance by powers beyond our grasp. When we seek our fortune, we venture out to expose ourselves to things beyond our control, but we also want to find out the story that will make sense of our lives – make sense of the fact that our lives are beyond our control. I had come to believe that this was the same paradox that lay at the root of happiness – or at least its etymological root: *happ* as chance events and random occurrences, *happ* as the fate that is determined in advance. A paradox that made it so hard to know where happiness lies: in that which others make happen to us and that we can never control, or in gaining the control that comes with discovering the story of our own lives.

This paradox, for me, is more than mere etymology: it is a reminder from the past, a memory preserved in a word, that happiness isn't what it had come to be defined as in the version of capitalism in which I lived. Happiness as a state you achieve by working hard on yourself: exercising, meditating, medicating. Optimising your functioning to make you a more efficient worker, a more reliable consumer. Happiness as something you work to achieve on your own. That lie has been told for many reasons, one of which is to make us forget that it is not the task of the isolated individual – something which doesn't even exist – but the community that we share to make life, if not happy, then at least bearable. My imagination, at least that summer, was smaller than the vast horizons of economic structures and social organisations. I was starting small; it was the best I could do. I wanted to find out if happiness, if I would find it at all, would only come to me through a similar mix of chance and fate. From opening myself to things beyond my control, from finding a way to tell this story of loss after the fact, in order to pass it on.

The fortune cookies I went to seek were part of a work of art called *Untitled (Fortune Cookie Corner)* created in 1990

by the Cuban-American artist Félix González-Torres, who
died of AIDS in 1995. It was first exhibited in Andrea Rosen
Gallery in New York. A mound of individually wrapped
fortune cookies was placed in the corner of the gallery, and
visitors were invited to take one, unwrap its shining foil,
read the message it contained and eat the sweet and crispy
cookie. The pile of cookies – which were simply bought
from any food store; it didn't matter where they came from
– were replenished for the month-long duration of the
original exhibition and then left to peter out when it closed.
González-Torres then set out of the core tenets according to
which this work of art could be exhibited again.

- The work can exist in more than one place at a time, as
  its uniqueness is defined by ownership.
- An intention of the work is that it can be manifested
  with ease.
- When the work is manifest, individuals must be
  permitted to choose to take pieces from the work.
- The owner (or authorised borrower) has the right to
  determine if and how the work is regenerated during
  the course of an exhibition/installation.
- The owner (or authorised borrower) has the right
  to interpret/choose the mode, configuration and
  placement of installation for each manifestation.
- The work exists even if it is not manifest.
- A manifestation of the work is only the work if it is
  installed by the owner or in the context of an authorised
  loan.
- An authorised manifestation of the work is the work
  and should only be referred to as the work.

That summer, the authorised borrowers of the work –
Andrea Rosen Gallery and David Zwirner Gallery – invited
one thousand people from all around the world to exhibit
between 240 and 1,000 fortune cookies at a location of their
choice on the 25th of May (like the work itself, they were quite
the controlling authorised borrowers). The exhibitors had to
replenish their piles back to the starting amount halfway
through the manifestation on June 14th. The manifestation
would end on July 5th, after which any cookies people hadn't
taken would cease to be 'the work'. It was left up to each
exhibitor to decide where to exhibit their cookies: whether it
would be somewhere the public could access or somewhere
private, intimate, hidden. It was also left to their discretion
(more precisely, the choice was given to them) whether they
wanted to reveal the location of their pile to the world by
uploading a photograph to a dedicated website.

After receiving an email announcing the beginning
of this exhibition, I began to check the website every day
to see if any of the sites would turn out to be in London.
After about a week, two locations appeared. The first was a
picture of a pile of red fortune cookies on a concrete block
in Trafalgar Square, installed by Joseph Kosuth. Kosuth,
one of the main theoreticians – and canniest promoters – of
conceptual art in the 1960s, had taught some of the early
members of the artist collective Group Material, which
González-Torres joined in 1987. With his creation of 'works'
like *Untitled (Fortune Cookie Corner)* that are more ideas and
instructions than physical objects, it's not hard to see why
Gonzalez-Torres saw himself as an 'extension' of aspects of
Kosuth's conceptualism, 'developing areas I think were not
totally dealt with'. The photograph showed quite a small

pile, and I was worried that all the cookies had already been taken. Kosuth, who had outlived his successor, had achieved enough not to have an email address you could find online, and, not presuming he would reply even if I could stalk him, I investigated the details of the second location.

This site was on Tennyson Road in Kilburn in north London, outside the house of the art critic Hettie Judah. Judah's email address I could track down, and I wrote to her asking if I could visit her house to see the work. She replied, kindly, saying that is, of course, fine, but that all the cookies from the first installation had already been taken. However, she added, she was due to replenish the pile that coming Sunday, and the afternoon would be a good time to come by as she would be at home, having a dinner party in the garden. I should come that Sunday, she warned, since if the fate of the first pile was anything to go by, the cookies would be gone in a couple of days.

As I set off on an hour-long cycle from Camberwell, where I lived, I wondered why my fellow Londoners were so acquisitive, greedy even. Were they also desperate for an omen of good fortune? The chance to encounter a work of art? Or just bored? On such a sunny Sunday, the parks and roads in the more residential areas outside the centre were full of people outside: walking, exercising, drinking, praying. Once I crossed the Thames at Waterloo Bridge, people disappeared. The inner core of London – Covent Garden, the West End, the City – was as vacant as it had been when the city was first locked down with the arrival of the Covid-19 pandemic in March. The lockdown had revealed how few people actually lived in central London: the streets I cycled through were nothing more than shuttered restaurants and empty offices. Roads that normally thronged were empty as I made my way across Oxford Street and up the Edgware Road, first laid out by the Romans two thousand years ago and now lined by Middle Eastern restaurants and shisha cafés, whose customers returned some life to the street the further out I cycled, towards Kilburn High Street, before turning off into a grid of Victorian terraced houses.

It wasn't so hard to figure out why someone would decide to exhibit *Untitled (Fortune Cookie Corner)* in the midst of the Covid-19 pandemic. It was the first of a series of 'candy pieces' that González-Torres conceptualised and exhibited in the early 1990s, all involving a pile of sweets, instructions for their installation and a similarly formatted name: *Untitled (USA Today)* (1990), *Untitled (Throat)* (1991). The instructions for *Untitled (Portrait of Ross)* (1991) and *Untitled Portrait of Ross in LA* (1991) stipulated that, ideally, the pile should be replenished daily, so its weight matched that of Ross Laycock, González-Torres's partner, who died of AIDS in 1991. *Untitled (Lover Boys)* (1991) had an ideal weight that matched that of González-Torres and Laycock together, or perhaps this should just be the weight of Félix and Ross, so intimate is the conception. After his death, González-Torres recorded that his 'remains were divided in a hundred small yellow envelopes of my lover's ashes – his last will'.

González-Torres designed candy pieces with a range of allusions to people and places. The pile in *Untitled (Portrait of Dad)* (1991) matched the weight of his father, *Untitled (Welcome Back Heroes)* (1991) was made of Bazooka bubble gum in an oblique memorialisation of the end of the first Gulf War. The series of works about Laycock, and González-

Torres's own subsequent death of AIDS, has however left an indelible mark on how these candy pieces are interpreted. To say that a work is 'about AIDS' is another loss the disease inflicts: an artist reduced to the suffering that fell upon them by chance. These candy pieces are about what it means to represent both that loss and that suffering. These are portraits that move from abundance to emptiness, the audience implicated in that disappearance through their consumption of the work of art. At the same time, they are portraits that expend themselves in the distribution of small moments of sweetness, a process that will go on as long as a world remains to carry out their instructions – as long a world exists to remember them.

Unforeseen disasters leave us grasping for precedents, scanning once more the stars or statistics for predictions we may have missed. In the early stages of the Covid-19 pandemic, these galleries were not alone in drawing comparisons with gay men's experience of the onset of HIV/AIDS in the early 1980s. All human contact was suspected as a risk, bodily fluids were vehicles of infection, and everyone was anxious about their status: positive or negative. I bristled at these comparisons. I felt like I was being granted expertise I had never sought. A lifetime of anxiety about the imbrication of intimacy and death wasn't justified by suddenly becoming relevant to the lives of the straight majority. And the act of comparison with gay men's past experiences obscured the reality that the HIV pandemic never ended and that its victims weren't only the white gay men assumed, silently, in these comparisons, but primarily now Black people and Black African women. The most these comparisons offered was the opportunity from some of the scabrous humour that has always been one way gay men have coped with the fate of HIV. After decades of not paying attention, it seems the world was about to learn some lessons from the gays. So among those Victorian houses, I wasn't only seeking my fortune. I was looking to see if the comparison, this time, would be different.

At first glance, Tennyson Road was an incongruous site for the exhibition of one of these candy pieces. Its residents had made the collective decision over time to paint the bay windows of the red-brick terraced houses various pastel colours so that the street was a parade of lilac, primrose and periwinkle blue. It was Victorian gentility gentrified into 21st-century gentility, a reminder of the iron grip on individual property that lies beneath the twee surface of the British middle class. Outside Judah's house, against a wall separating her garden from the footpath, a pile of fortune cookies in gold and red foil stood piled on a low wooden table. I sat down on the kerb of the opposite side of the street, tired from my cycle and curious to witness the response to this shining invitation.

Although it was a quiet street, it was a warm summer's day, and it wasn't long until people out for a Sunday stroll began to walk past the pile of fortune cookies. The first I saw were a father and daughter walking what looked like an expensively groomed grey poodle. The father, muscled like a City banker, was wearing a clear plastic face shield. The daughter, blonde, skipped in a white dress. As she passed the table, she proclaimed to the dog in a sing-song voice, 'We don't pick it up, it's not good, we don't want corona', revelling, as children so easily can, in policing the rules imposed upon them.

As I continued to wait, sitting across the street, a few more couples – always men and women – passed by. Some stopped to inspect the pile of cookies, but nobody took one. Finally, I heard a man, I'd guess in his fifties, say to his wife: 'Maybe it's a corona trap?' They had passed me by, and, unable to see his face, I couldn't tell whether he was making a wry joke or revealing a shared, well-heeled suspicion towards the invitation to try something strange, to participate, to accept an unknown pleasure or just towards art itself.

If no one took a cookie, I wondered, would this work have somehow failed? The question felt like asking if the tree really fell in the forest if no one was there to witness its fall. I thought again about the instructions. 'When the work is manifest, individuals must be permitted to choose to take pieces from the work.' There was no compulsion here, unlike in other kinds of participatory art, where the requirement to take part can feel controlling, subjecting yourself to an artist's fantasy of social engineering. Not just permitted, 'permitted to choose'. These words seemed carefully chosen. People can exercise their choice, and the possibility of rejection is accepted. This was less permission than an invitation, one that assumed you had agency, perhaps the kind of agency often lacking in life: the ability to say no and to have that respected. But an invitation to what?

It was an invitation to choose to be part of 'the work'. By eating a cookie, the work would enter your body and, in trace elements, stay there, maybe forever. (This might be the glucose that your cells use to repair that damaged patch of liver, worn out from all that drinking.) The work might seem to disappear, but in fact, you were preserving

its memory, invisibly, in your body for as long as you lived.
And in preserving that memory, you would become part of a
collective, a crowd that exists in the bodies of strangers who
have already eaten a cookie and those who will consume
one in future. It is a community defined neither by space
nor time, potentially infinite. You could become part of
this work by choosing pleasure – the simple sweet joy of a
fortune cookie – and at the same time, you would become
part of the work by enacting loss. The whittling away of the
pile and the larger loss behind them: the death of a lover, the
tragedy of AIDS. You would become part of a community
in which sweetness and loss, pleasure and suffering, cannot
be untangled. To be part of this community would be to
remember they never could, that it is the experience of
shared suffering that binds us together, and that there is a
sad sweetness that comes from this assumption of solidarity.
The body – its appetites, its damage – is what makes you a
member of this crowd, yet it is a strange body, at once visceral
and abstract, one lacking any identifying features other than
its experience of desire and pain. A community unbounded
by space and time, transcending visible differences while
remaining true to the body's desire.

After half an hour sitting on the footpath, I became
worried I might begin to attract attention (it was that kind
of area), so I got up, crossed the road and began taking
photographs of the pile of cookies. Seeing me from inside,
Judah waved and came out, saying she had remembered my
email. I asked her how people have been responding to her
pile and why she thought they had disappeared so quickly
when it seemed to me, on the basis of a little fieldwork, that
people seemed reluctant to even touch them. She said she

had noticed that people took far more at night than during the day. Once she saw a man come and stuff handfuls into a carrier bag. 'Well,' she concluded, 'I have people in my garden, so I have to go. I hope it was worth the cycle.'

Alone on the street, I finally did what I had come to do. I squatted, hesitated and grabbed. Looking at the shiny red and gold wrapper in my hand, I noticed it had an expiration date: 28th February 2022. Did that mean its power of prediction only lasted so long? Something about that expiration date and the sounds of a dinner party to which I wasn't invited combined to drown me in a wave of bathos. This wasn't where I wanted to know my fortune. This wasn't the moment where I wanted to choose to believe. I decided to prolong the mystery – forestall the disappointment – and to wait until I had my second cookie and open both together. I was still hedging my bets. This was precisely why I was seeking my fortune – that near impossibility of giving up control.

According to the photograph I had seen online, Kosuth had installed his pile of cookies on top of a concrete box in front of the National Gallery in Trafalgar Square. By now, it was midday and hot. Luckily my ride back to the centre of London was all downhill, and the breeze helped lift me out of my bathos. In the absence of traffic, I cycled down roads I never before would have dared to take on a bike. I went around the massive roundabout at Marble Arch, down the wide expanse of Park Lane to the Wellington monument and then up through Piccadilly. I experienced, for the first time, the impression these monuments and avenues were intended to have when, at the beginning of the 19th century, they were laid out to provide England with a capital worthy of an Empire. Military might and the glorification of violence curving in one arc right through the heart of London and culminating, like the tip of a sabre, at Trafalgar Square.

Arriving at the plaza in front of the National Gallery, I passed a van giving out food to homeless people, overseen by a group of Metropolitan Police. When I arrived at the place where the concrete box should have been, it wasn't there. I opened the photograph on my phone, comparing the view I was seeing to the view on my screen, but the concrete box seemed to disappear in the passage from reproduction to reality. I eventually realised that what looked like roadblocks on the side of the plaza must have been the concrete boxes, but they were now covered in plastic barriers that made their surface inaccessible. I wandered around to see if the cookies had been moved elsewhere, but I soon gave up. The site intended for the work no longer existed.

That wasn't the first time I had been to Trafalgar Square that summer. Three weeks earlier, I had stood there with some friends at a demonstration organised by Black Lives Matter UK. The immediate trigger for the demonstration had been the murder of George Floyd and Breonna Taylor by police in the United States, and the disproportionate amount of Black people, like the transport worker Belly Mujinga, who were dying during the Covid-19 pandemic in the UK. The larger, longer-term causes were revealed by the signs we passed as we joined the crowd assembling outside the Houses of Parliament. 'How Many More Deaths in Police Custody?' 'The UK Is Not Innocent.' 'Teach Black History.' 'Stop Killing the Mandem, Galdem and Transdem.' As we walked up Whitehall, a street rebuilt at the end of the 19th century to house the administration of the British Empire at its peak, I noticed that the statues lining the middle of the road had been covered in cladding. War heroes who killed in the service of Empire and the nurses who tended to them; Earl Haig, who ordered mass killings in Sudan; and Earl Kitchener, who administered concentration camps in South Africa – all were now protected behind grey plastic. I wondered whether these statues had been hidden out of fear or shame until it hit me that those were the inextricable reasons they had been erected in the first place.

My friends and I stayed at the outskirts of the protest, whose organisers had gathered in front of the National Gallery. Towards the end, groups of Black Londoners rose higher in the crowd to lead chants of 'No Justice, No Peace, No Racist Police'. As I watched, I realised they were standing on the concrete boxes upon which Kosuth had previously decided to exhibit his cookies. The Metropolitan Police must have also covered them in cladding to protect them, worried about the fate of concrete, just like that of statues.

I never figured out what happened to this pile of cookies. Were they swept away by the police? The crowd? Neither? Did some remain to be taken away by the protesters? Even had some remained, would they have cared?

A single fortune cookie in one hand, my bike wheeled by the other, I decided to walk back across the river and have a drink on the South Bank as the sun set. I wanted to introduce a little ceremony: it was time to discover my fortune. I peeled off the foil, cracked it open and pulled out a scroll of paper: 'Behind every successful man stands an amazed woman.'

I decided to give up control. What could make this fortune come true?

* * *

Nine months earlier, I had stood on the South Bank in search
of an amazed woman. I had gone to visit *Kiss My Genders*,
an exhibition of art that played with representations of
gender, sexuality and desire. It was heavy on photography
– it seemed to assume that representation was first and
foremost a visual matter – and contained the work of artists
like Ajamu X, Peter Hujar, Juliana Huxtable and Zanele
Muholi. With no disrespect intended to these artists, many
of whom I had long loved, the person whose work I had
come to see was Catherine Opie. I saw her name listed in
an announcement, but not the works of hers that would
be on show. I was hoping to finally see in person a series
of photographs that had long fascinated me: *Self-Portrait
(Cutting)* (1993), *Self-Portrait (Pervert)* (1994), and *Self-Portrait
(Nursing)* (2004). I went round and around the concrete halls
of the Hayward Gallery to no avail. The only portraits by
Opie on display were portraits of others: members of the
queer community in San Francisco where Opie lived in the
1990s. *Mike and Sky* (1993) showed two of Opie's friends –
bearded, muscled and tattooed against a purple background
– who were the first in her circle to start taking testosterone
and to live as men. *Justin Bond* (1993) showed another friend,
again against a regal indigo backdrop, in pearls and pussy-
bow like an elegant housewife, yet cinched and bound in
a corset. My fascination remained frustrated. As I left, I
saw two photographs by Opie that I had never seen before.
Photographs of the ocean, taken from a tanker as it circled
the globe.

For all the dignity they accord to their sitters through formal allusions to Renaissance paintings of royalty, Opie's photographs of friends like Mike, Sky and Justin were intended to offer more than portraits of specific people. When asked in a 1996 interview, 'were you consciously setting out to represent a community, rather than individual people', Opie replied, 'Yeah, I thought of it as a community. My investment in the community is very important to the work. In fact, I probably wouldn't have done the work if I hadn't felt that I didn't like the way my community was being represented in the world.' Ten years later, she emphasised the same point. 'I was trying to represent communities that weren't being represented, but also in a way to create that representation.' Her portraits are more than representations of a particular community in time and space. They are also about the process by which any community comes into being – perhaps only comes into being – by acquiring a collective representation of itself. And they are about one way that community can be remembered: by making them visible forever, by making the world see the difference of their bodies.

Although I was disappointed not to see the photographs I sought, the exhibition did leave me struck by a difference: how Opie used portraits to accord dignity to others but to debase herself. *Self-Portrait (Cutting)* shows Opie from the back, from the waist up, against a turquoise brocade background. Her hair is short, she is wearing lots of earrings, and a tattoo circles her right arm. Across the soft expanse of her back, a child-like drawing is freshly carved into her skin. It shows two stick women holding hands in front of a house, under a sun emerging from behind a cloud. Her flesh has been freshly cut; blood oozes down the side of the house and from one woman's skirt. It is a fantasy of two women living in domestic bliss, of two lesbians living heterosexuality's illusory image of itself. It is a fantasy that has been scored into the body by someone else since Opie could not have carved this drawing into her own back. It is someone else's fantasy that has been imprinted upon Opie's body. It is a fantasy that wounds and will leave a scar.

Self-Portrait (Pervert) shows Opie from the front against a black-and-gold fabric backdrop. Her face is still invisible: she is wearing a black leather gimp mask. Again she is topless, her hands crossed on her lap, resting on leather chaps, and both arms, from shoulders down to wrists, are pierced with syringe needles. The word 'Pervert', displayed like a crest above two decorative branches, is freshly carved into her chest. The source of this wound is more ambiguous. At first glance, it seems it must have been cut by someone else, so neatly intricate are the bloody lines. Just like a self-portrait, however, it could also have been drawn by Opie sitting in front of a mirror. Its author could have been the other outside us or the other within that reveals itself when we look into a mirror. Whatever its origin, in this photograph, an insult intended to wound has become a source of pride. Opie has embraced the insult's intention to rob her of her individuality, humanity and identity. She is proud to display her anonymous, perverted body. Even more: you get the sense she enjoys it.

Self-Portrait (Nursing) shows Opie in the same pose, ten years later. Seated, topless from the waist up, against a scarlet-and-gold brocade backdrop. In this photograph, her face is finally visible. We see her rich red cheeks, the pimples on her nose, her dark eyebrows. Her gaze looks down at the blonde baby boy she is cradling in her arms. The baby is suckling on her left nipple, pulling taut the flesh of her breasts and stretching white scars still visible from a decade before when someone else was incising into that body.

There were photographs I had wanted to see in the flesh because that was where they showed life was lived. We are not brains in a jar; we are not immortal souls; we are not an unconscious without history. We are our bodies. Our desires, our sense of self, our identity – these are not conceptual abstractions but bleeding, scarred, pimpled things. Not visceral but the viscera itself. I felt I needed to see these images on photographic paper, attuned to the level of my eyes, in relationship to the dimensions of my own body. Instead, before and after that exhibition, I had only ever seen them on screens or in library books, reproduced to the wrong size. What I was also missing, scrolling numbly on my laptop, was the experience these photographs seemed to offer of photography itself as a wound. Photography – analogue photography – is a mark made by light on paper. It is a stain, a burning, a bleaching. It is an act of human interference that makes the world wound itself. And the print made from the negative is a kind of scar, the remnant from the original exposure. These pictures of cutting and healing showed photography as made in the flesh, and I wanted to get so close I could almost touch.

In the flesh. These are photographs that show what the body can bear, what, as in the process of photography itself, matter can make visible. In *Self-Portrait (Cutting)*, an image of lesbian life is imprinted on Opie's body by somebody else. This is a life where being in a relationship with a woman is

no different – can be imagined to be different – from that
of the normal, property-owning, heterosexual couple. This
image hurts, literally. Opie has a kind of blunt genius in
making abstract psychic processes literal, and, in this case,
it is the process of having your identity imposed upon you
from without. *This is what it means to be a lesbian.* This process
leaves a mark forever. What this photograph also shows is
the demand, coming from without, that identity be made
visible on the body: that the body shows on the surface the
kind of desires hidden inside. *Show me what you want.* This
is the demand put upon all kinds of bodies: the limp wrist is
the sign of the faggot; the buzz cut hair that of the dyke. And
it is not just a demand to make same-sex desire visible. His
spread legs are a billboard for the straight man; her crossed
ones an advertisement for what he will possess. (Even
while seating, heterosexuality always defines the woman
in relation to the man.) Her face hidden, Opie's photograph
shows just how impersonal these demands are. Who needs
our body to reveal who and how we want to fuck? Who
wants to see our scars?

We do, proclaim the subjects of Opie's portraits. *We
perverts.* If *Self-Portrait (Cutting)* shows a wound definitively
imposed from without, the wound in *Self-Portrait (Pervert)*
could have been carved by Opie herself, in front of a mirror
– *this is what I want others to see* – or by someone who, when
cutting into her chest, would have had to look Opie in the
eye – *let's tell the world who we are!* This self-portrait glories
in being wounded. Blood here is not an index of damage but
raw material for rubies. This photograph shows the pleasure
one can take in being wounded, a pleasure as rich and
complex as the fabric brocade that folds around its subject. It

refutes the assumption that to have one's identity imposed from without can only be a source of pain. Just as the masochist enjoys being cut and pierced, so too the body can take pleasure in being identified, defined and made visible by someone else. The pleasure can come from the power and control that one gains from submitting to the sadist's blows, the bottom coming out on top, as bottoms always do. It can also come from the way wounding enables the formation of the community that Opie set out to depict. A slur, intended to brand an outcast, becomes a visible badge of pride, enabling the perverts to find each other, come together and strap each other, lovingly, into leather, chains and masks. A wound becomes a scar, pain transforms into a permanent memorial, and perhaps it's this permanence that draws us to forming communities around our scars. Real scars never fade; if we build our worlds upon them, we hope that neither will they.

The self-portrait makes another psychic process literal, visible and embodied; one described in an essay published the same year, as if by chance, that Opie was having 'pervert' tenderly carved into her chest. For the theorist Wendy Brown, political identities in the age of global neoliberal capitalism have come to be formed by what she calls 'wounded attachments'. When a group of outcasts – queers, fags, dykes, *perverts* – reclaim an identity that was created to exclude them, that identity becomes 'premised on this exclusion for its very existence as identity'. By doing so, 'it installs pain . . . in the very foundation of its political claim, in its demand for recognition as identity'. We become attached to our wounds because our wounds become what we are – at least in the realm of politics, the realm where we try to act with others. We desire – or are we made to desire? – our pain. Brown's worry is what to do with this masochistic attachment to pain. What possibility for collective transformation does this attachment to individual suffering enable or foreclose? She sees the same possibility as Opie, the masochist – that the attachment to wounding shows our capacity for pleasure as much as suffering. She asks, 'What if it were possible to rehabilitate the memory of desire within identificatory processes, the moment in desire [. . .] prior to its wounding and thus prior to the formation of identity at the site of the wound?' What if, that is, we gave as much weight to our desire to attach as to our susceptibility to wound since bodies will always bleed? What if the memory of desire, rather than wounds, could build a community, one that doesn't require the permanence of a scar but that draws people together in pursuit of a shared vision of pleasure, a collective quality of desire?

This, it seemed, was my fortune. To find Cathy, a woman amazed by the beauty of the community that pain can form, behind Félix's pile of fortune cookies. Inside the work of one artist, generating sweetness and suffering out of chance encounters, was another, obtaining pleasure and control by submitting to pain. But this could only be my fortune because I wanted it to be. Only I could transform a randomly chosen phrase, meaningless in itself, into a story that linked events across a year in my life. I was the one who wanted there to be a connection between these two artists, even if it took a cookie to reveal my own desire to me – another lesson in how we never really know what we want. Faced with a world of suffering, I had wanted there to be a reason behind that phrase. I had wanted there to be a story, and my desire to believe was so strong it created one.

Stories are the way we deal with chance; stories are a sign we can't deal with chance. We find it unbearable that things just happen, for good or ill, with no rhyme or reason, cause or care. That things are beyond our control. And so, we seek out patterns in the stars, correspondences in cards, fortune in cookies after dinner. Or in no less of a form of magical thinking, we turn to stories, plots and narratives when faced with suffering, pain, and loss. Not just 'this is happening for a reason', but knowing, hallucinating, that a reason is out there enables us to keep on going. But also: something is making this happen. Rather the fantasy of someone's power over us than the reality of a world that inflicts loss beyond what we could ever control.

This was my fortune, the story I created. Two artists creating worlds where desire leads to suffering. When love between men is followed by generations of death, when love between women draws a lifetime of scars. The drama in this story, the conflict demanding resolution, was that their responses were as different as they were similar. For Félix, participation in loss, through taking candy into your body, is the condition for a more complex understanding of joy: that desire and loss are always intertwined; that by devouring what we want, we make it disappear. For Cathy, a more complicated wrestling with pain: that we can enjoy pain, that learning to enjoy it can be a way to master it but one that leaves us needing our pleasures to leave us marked and scarred. For Félix, suffering is not shown, whether because its magnitude can never be represented, or to avoid repeating by representing the loss, to refuse to provide evidence or proof. For Cathy, the pain must be made visible. The world needs to see how much heterosexuality hurts, and she will restage it, relive it, at the cost of scarring her body for life.

Their responses provided two models for the communities these experiences of desire and suffering can form. For Félix, the community's bodies are never visibly represented. They remain abstract yet fully material. What they have in common is not so much an identity as the fact that, for one moment in time, they shared an appetite, a desire. This community is theoretically infinite, immortal, bounded only by the execution of the concept's instructions. For Cathy, these bodies in all their particularity are the only thing that is represented; the body is all there is. We see what has marked individual bodies, we see them bleed, and we see them scar, which is to say they change through ageing. These bodies are finite, as are the communities they form. They must reproduce, creating body out of body, life out of life.

Yet, both show communities can only be formed if we remember others, whether by incorporating that memory in our bodies or displaying it in pictures to be seen by future eyes. These were two artists who created different memorials to desire: sweets and scars. They wanted to preserve the memory of their desires because if they didn't no one else would, and because their desires, and the suffering that came with them, were so new in the world. These new desires didn't come from a story that had already been told or from filling in a lack, a fate they could never escape. Through becoming art, their desire brought something new into the world, something worth remembering, even if it's the memory of loss and pain. And if we want to call that desire queer, their art shows that we should treasure the tension between memory and invention that queerness has at its heart. That precisely because it doesn't have a fixed legacy, a fully defined inheritance, it can always be a way to name desires that are new. But to be able to name what is new, it must find a way to remember that prevents memory becoming a script, a pattern: a fate.

And maybe they show what art and desire have in common. Both can expose us to chance and bring newness into the world. But mere novelty isn't enough to change the world. Neither sweets nor scars can topple statues. Queerness, with its lack of memories and novel desires, is a fragile thing. You need to know how little to expect from it in order for it to make you happy.

Félix/Cathy; Man/woman; gay/lesbian; of colour/ white; abstract/material; invisible/visible; concept/ photograph; transient/scarred. The oppositions and similarities piled up, demanding a resolution. But that is what a belief in art or stories can never really offer.

The year after he first exhibited *Untitled (Fortune Cookie Corner)*, González-Torres designed a candy piece called *Untitled (Placebo)* (1991), whose instructions specified an ideal weight, his heaviest thus far, of a thousand pounds of silver-wrapped cookies. Was it an abundance of hope or a crushing mass? He designed a second, lighter work called *Untitled (Blue Placebo)* (1991) and his final ever candy piece, his farewell to this art form he invented, was *Untitled (Landscape – Placebo – for Roni)* (1993): over a thousand pounds of candies wrapped in gold. A placebo makes for a strange gift: to a friend, Roni or to a viewer. A placebo is a substance or treatment that is designed intentionally to produce no healing effect in a sick body. Placebos, in the form of sugar pills, are often required to be administered in trials to test the efficacy of medicine, especially those developed to treat new and as yet incurable diseases. For the trial to be effective, patients – participants – cannot know whether they have received the medicine or the placebo. Placebos, in one sense, are cruel. At the same time, the placebo effect in medical trials is well attested and, in some cases, clinically effective. People will heal simply by believing they have been given a cure. Placebos, in this sense, offer hope of a kind. *Untitled (Fortune Cookie Corner)* and the story I made from it: maybe both were nothing more than a placebo. Like the fortune the work contained, the community it promised, the power of the story, if it was to have any, lies in our belief, our desire, our delusion. The stories created by works of art need protection from the crowds that assemble in the world. That fragility, when placed into the real streets of the city, outside the gallery walls, is a reminder there is as much cruelty as hope in that belief.

As that year came to an end, art galleries briefly opened only to close once more, and international travel remained largely impossible, and so I never got to see Opie's photographs in the flesh by visiting collections abroad. This was another reminder: these are portraits of beautiful perverts, but they are also expensive commodities, hoarded in vaults and private homes, inaccessible to any community except the rich or those to whom they grant access, like medieval royalty, through donating their work as an act of charity, or perhaps pity, to a museum. Instead, I spent the winter looking at exhibitions of Opie's work online. I discovered she had exhibited new work that summer in a gallery in Los Angeles. Her focus and subjects had changed. Not portraits of people but of the Okefenokee swamp, originally in Miccosukee and Seminole land, and now dispossessed into the states of south Georgia and north Florida. As far as I could see through the anaesthetic blue glow of my laptop screen, these swamps were thick with life. Vegetation decomposed into water, water nourishing new vegetation These wetlands are part of a broader ecosystem through which the environment across the southern Gulf Coast regulates itself against flooding and drought. The photographs were accompanied by a series of digital collages composed of images Opie had clipped from magazines: displaced people entering the United States, Black Lives Matter protestors, guns, Donald Trump. For decades, corporations have been attempting to mine the titanium and zirconium deposits that lie beneath the Okefenokee swamps, only to have been resisted thus far by protests and collective community pressure on public authorities. That year, the Trump Administration removed federal protection from part of the swamplands, opening it up to new mining operations. Opie had turned to wounds that hurt us all, damage no individual can heal, caused as they are by another kind of collective desire, the capitalism that remained beyond my imaginative horizon.

The only resolution is the story itself. That is what we seek – the plot revealing it was all meant to be, that it wasn't all just chance. Seeking, desiring, wanting to believe: that is our impossible fate. We can never see life's pattern in advance. We can only create it when we have decided that something has come to an end or when what we have been seeking reveals it has come to an end with us. I still wanted to believe in the possibility of happiness, but I knew now that this was a desire, not fate. I would always be a lover. Such, I could now tell myself, was my fortune.

The story makes happen what never really could: people meeting across space and time, dead artists speaking to the living, our happiness something that was meant to be. The story is the resolution, the placebo and the scar. It makes us happy only because we believe; it heals by covering up what lies beneath. The chance occurrence, pain without meaning, suffering without resolution – all that just happens.

LOOKING LIKE WOLFGANG

In 1987, the year I was born, Wolfgang Tillmans, then aged 19, drew his own portrait. With pencil, he outlined a long face with high cheekbones, slightly angled to the left, with small but plump lips, piercing, narrowed eyes and a lock of hair that fell down the middle of his forehead. Then he drew a second self-portrait: this time in profile, his head and shoulders turning back over his left shoulder. This almost looks like a different person. A squat, compressed face, a square forehead and a pointed, hooked nose. Etched lines score shade all over the side of his face. Only the narrowed eyes, looking back at the viewer, seem the same. Then he photocopied this drawing, the nuances of pencil becoming a matt black, a ghostly stain of grey shadow rising up from his shoulder.

That same year he posed for a black-and-white photograph. He is standing on a single bed, leaning against a wall, wearing only white trousers, his chest flecked with blood. It wasn't enough to draw himself, nor to turn that drawing, traced by his own hand, into a mechanically reproduced copy. To create a portrait of himself, Tillmans betrayed the impulse that he would later describe as driving him to become a photographer: 'I take pictures in order to see the world.' He needed a photograph in order to see himself.

Do we create because we lack? He must have needed to see himself as an image, a likeness, because up until that age, he had never met someone who looked like him. Who really looked like him, who shared what he felt inside, his desire to be with other men. Or rather, who he could be sure looked like him since someone who deals in portraits knows how much can be hidden under appearances. Maybe what he was missing, from parents, from friends, was someone to whom he could say – You look like me! And someone who could recognise him back and say – I look like you! These photographs and drawings seem unsure as to whether this experience was especially damaging or unique. The teenager has shown himself daubed with blood; the neutral repetition of the photocopier simply notes – this is just how things are. This experiment with various forms of self-portraiture suggests he wondered what effect this kind of upbringing had on him, would have had on anyone. To spend so long without ever believing you have seen someone like you – what a desire to find someone who does that must have fostered, what a scepticism about the very possibility must have been left in its wake.

Here is a different kind of portrait. Wolfgang Tillmans was born in 1968 in Remscheid, a small city in Nordrhein-

Westphalia, Germany. In 1987, he moved to Hamburg, where he had his first solo photography exhibitions. In 1990, he moved to England and studied at Bournemouth College of Art and Design. In 1992, he moved again to London, and since then, apart from a year spent in New York from 1994 and 1995, he has lived and worked in London and Berlin. He has held over 150 solo exhibitions; he has designed and published over 30 books of photography.

The first things Tillmans photographed were the planets in the sky: the moon, the sun and a lunar eclipse. At 18, using a laser photocopier, he began making copies of pictures he found. He bought his first camera, a Contax single-lens reflex, when he was 20 and living in Hamburg, and began taking photographs of nightlife and people in clubs, something he continued when he moved to England, and soon he was publishing pictures in fashion magazines like *i-D*. The world Tillmans took pictures in order to see turn out to contain so much: dancers in night clubs, bowls of fruit, erections, the epiglottis, computer cables, the haze of light in a summer park, the breaking of a wave . . .

I first came across Wolfgang Tillmans when I was aged 19 in the year 2007, in the pink pages of *BUTT* magazine. *BUTT* was a self-proclaimed 'international faggot magazine for interesting homosexuals and the men who love them'. These men were nothing like those in the gay magazines I had travelled for an hour on the bus to the next town over to furtively browse as a teenager: *Attitude, Gay Times, Him*. These men were tanned, muscled, hairless and, above all, shiny. The interesting homosexuals in *BUTT* were skinny, pale, hairy, chubby, tattooed, curvy and bearded. They wore sports clothes, torn jeans and ripped underwear; though, often they wore nothing at all. These bodies looked sticky: with stubble, sweat and cum. I soon began collecting as many back issues as I could. Tillmans, I learned, had defined that look since the magazine's first issue. He shot the cover of issue 16, an image that, for me, summed up the look *BUTT* offered. On a metal table in a messy kitchen, a soft chubby boy with blue eyes sits with his knees pulled into his chest and his hands around his shins, wearing nothing but a chain, white trainers and socks, and white underwear pulled down to his knees revealing his asshole reflected against the surface of the table. Smiling, tender, funny, the subject of a visual joke, not at all serious – and soft.

Issue 19 featured the magazine's first two photographs of Tillmans himself. The first was a portrait of him aged 20, standing in Adidas swimming trunks beside an outdoor pool in Hamburg. I was 19, I was soon going to be 20, I had Adidas swimming trunks, and I had even been to an outdoor pool in Hamburg. These coincidences couldn't just be chance. There had to be some meaning in the way age and image were repeated. I wanted there to be, even if then I didn't then know why. I wanted to go home and wear those trunks in front of a mirror, to imitate his look, shy and louche at the same time. The second was of Tillmans as he was then, aged 38. He is wearing a t-shirt with the logo of a San Francisco bar called 'The Hole in the Wall', army camouflage pants and black boots. He is surrounded by people drinking in the park, and he is smiling. The photograph was nothing special, but what entranced me was the ordinariness of it all; how ordinary it was for him to be content in a crowd. How obvious it was to say, in the interview, that he lives in 'a historical moment that has nothing to do with gay assimilation, trying to be hetero, family values'. That he could also say: 'I'm interested in values . . . I'm convinced that what we do matters…that what I do in my everyday life and my work does matter.' That is what and where I wanted to be, drinking a can in a sunny park, maybe London or Berlin. The photograph was an image of my future. How to get there? How could I join that we? The blithe confidence of being able to state what he had achieved in his work: 'my personal utopia as reality succeeded.' I wanted to see that utopia. I wanted to look like Wolfgang.

* * *

Interrail (1987). An A4 sheet of paper, landscape, displays a black and white photocopied image. A young man is asleep on a seat, leaning against a wall. His legs, bent at the knee, fill up the bottom left of the picture. Behind his head, leaning back in a corner of shadow, is a curtain that frames a window, which lets in light all along the right of the image. The man is asleep in a rail carriage, taken in the year I was born. Did he ever know this photograph was taken? For when we are sleeping, at our most vulnerable, we cannot know what we look like.

The following year, 2008, when I was interrailing around Europe, I saw an exhibition of Tillmans' work for the first time in Berlin. It was held in the Hamburger Bahnhof, once a train terminal and now the city's contemporary art museum. It wasn't what I was expecting. It didn't look like any photography exhibition I had seen before. Nothing was framed. The photographs were fixed to the wall with thumbtacks or held up with wires and claps. They were scattered all over the walls in different sizes, some as small as a postcard, some larger than me. Some were in clusters; some were in strict lines. In one sequence of rooms, long vitrines covered in glass displayed long tables of photocopies from books and magazines about technology, AIDS, cars, refugees and aeroplanes. I spent the afternoon in the museum bookstore, which because of the exhibition was stacked with books and catalogues about his work. I learned that Tillmans designed and installed each exhibition himself, photographing his installations as works of art. Photographs of previous exhibitions revealed that Tillmans displays the same photographs over and over again, each time alongside different combinations of images. And that he shows the same images in exhibitions, in photobooks and magazines. What mattered was not the individual photograph. What matters are the relationships an image can have.

Arkadia I (1996). A black and white photograph: three men hold one another, faces resting in shoulders, so that of two of them you only see the surface of their heads. One, to the left, has tousled hair and wears a denim jacket. A second, to the right, has short fair hair and is in sportswear. The third's face appears in profile, facing downwards, across the front of the image. He is wearing a brown raincoat, has short brown hair that curls a little on top, thick eyebrows and a chin, just like mine, that is a little too small and looks better in stubble. His eyes are closed, and he smiles. The three men suspend one another, embracing and embraced – or rather, the three boys, since here they have lifted themselves out of ageing, out of time.

Why did I feel that was I was seeing was some kind of utopia? Some of it was simple; to state, not to achieve. In the first two decades of his photographs, from the early 90s into the new millennium, people never really appeared to work, or work was only creation: playing music, designing clothes and taking photographs. It was a world without any evident fear of sex. AIDS appeared only in the form of a memorial statue or in photographs from 1992. Everything is worthy of attention: socks on the floor, plants growing on a city balcony, the surface of a pool. Anything is beautiful if you can find the right way to see it, and you will, because someone will always be there to show you how to see things differently. If you follow these photographs over the years, you see the same names and faces appear: Alex, Lutz, Suzanne, Christoph, Isa, Conor. A world where what is constant is not the single romantic lover but a whole network of friends. And even though, by the time I saw them, these photographs belonged in the past, they seemed to offer an image of the future: this is what human life could be like. After the fall of the Berlin Wall, when history seemed fated to offer nothing more than a deeper, wider version of capitalist commodification, here at least was a world that could be transformed by human relationships: by sex, friendship, tenderness and care.

It was a utopia where you could be intimate anywhere. On a dancefloor, a man holds a woman's hair as her face tilts back in ecstasy. Two men, covered in sweat, kiss each other so furiously their faces are invisible. That the photo is cropped to show only this means they could be anyone, and they could be anywhere. A woman stands in a field, wearing only a jacket, displaying her vulva for a man to inspect, curiously. There seemed to be no boundaries in this world, no division of space into public and private, no sense of some places allowing some things, but not others. To be intimate means to be close to someone; to intimate means to make known. This was a utopia in which both meanings were forever fused. You could be close to anyone; you will always be known. It was a world so fantastic that even its description feels like an act of imagination.

shiny shorts (2002). A rectangular photograph, upright, shows an upside-down close up of a skinny man's stomach, crotch and thighs, cut off at the top of the image just below the knee. He is wearing nothing but a pair of shiny blue sports shorts with a white trim and band down the side. He is lying on a green sofa, a pair of discarded jeans to his right. Beneath the shorts, you can see a bulge but nothing more than a faint outline. What you see is what you would really want to touch: the shimmering folds of the fabric, those synthetic threads that feel softer than silk.

If you can be intimate anywhere, that thing we call sexuality slips out of its frame. Feelings and desires don't belong to particular spaces and places; they don't attach to identifiable bodies. The impulse to lick someone's armpit doesn't have to be restrained based on where you are. You can experience that delicious slither of wind between your ass or across your nipples lying on any surface of the Earth. You can feel reborn on a Sunday morning at a leaking nightclub urinal. Shorts: you can always wear comfortable shorts. Precisely because nothing has to be tied to any one place, the body's sensations can connect to things as if for the first time. This is what a tree feels like between my legs. This is what your sweat tastes like at three in the afternoon. If our desires aren't divided into public and private, inside and outside, neither are we. Tillmans has said that in his photographs, 'sexuality is located on the surface of the clothes'. It isn't something hidden, something given the sweet sting of suppression. It is something that can always be seen.

I found it funny, as I began to get to know Tillmans' work, that I was becoming obsessed with a photographer. I had never owned a camera. After a few early fumbles, as awkward as a rejected crush, I deleted social media and have never used it since. I own no photographs, I've never bought a mirror, and I wipe every image from my phone about once a year. Just like my grandmother, who refused to have her photograph taken, I have never liked what I have looked like photographed.

I never found out why she hated being photographed. That was the kind of thing she would never have told me. So I'll never know if she also looked at photographs of herself and thought: I don't remember that happening. How could I? No one can see themselves like that, not as a reflection, but from the outside. If she felt those frozen images of herself seen by someone else began to displace her memory of what that person was seeing, what it was like to be that person seeing. That is something a photograph could never show because she lived her life in time's endless flow.

If she also thought that the only way to make sense of a photograph was to find out who took it, since that is what a portrait shows: what someone looked like, for an instant, to someone else. If she also made sense of photographs by putting them back into time: turning them into stories, subjecting them to the act of remembering in order to prevent them from falsifying memory. Or if she just looked at herself and thought: that's not what I look like. Not what I think I look like, anyway.

I didn't want Wolfgang Tillmans – I wouldn't have said no, but I imagine it would have been a comic fumble, one getting off much later than the other, concluding in a blush of friendly, if rueful, disappointment. Nor, since I've always been fascinated by photography from a starting point of unease, did I want to be him – I would hate the burden of taking photographs for a living. It was a need, a desire, coming from wanting something that was missing, but its goal wasn't possession, the determined targeting that for me is pure lust. So I wasn't living a tragic little novella of obsession. I simply wanted to look like him: not just the hair, the clothes, but the posture, the ease. Was that more a drama of aspiration? Transformation? Imitation? I didn't know what I was doing because I didn't know what kind of story this was.

I didn't know the plot, but I knew at least part of the motivation: I wanted to look like him because I wanted to belong to his world. The look, then, was a means to an end. Yet I didn't know my end, the conclusion to my story. I didn't know my genre. Closet drama or universal epic? The drama: gay men are rarely brought up by someone they can believe looks like them. The first sting of shame comes from being told what you look like. I don't know, that looks a little gay, don't you think? Discovering that there is model for who others say you are, and untangling that from who you want to be, becomes a solo performance in five long acts. Although isn't this the universal epic we all live? Doesn't everyone want to look like the object of someone else's desire? How else will you be loved?

Or was my genre the proverb: 'you need to see it to be it'? And not the kind of proverb that distils the hard-won wisdom of centuries, but the kind dredged up from a swamp of self-help books, spiritual gurus and motivational speeches for corporate success, whose tone is celebratory and sinister. Achieving your dreams, manifesting your intention, becoming the real you: the self becomes a task, a labour, an achievement, and achievements must be rewarded. With love, money and success, ideally the fusion of all three. Banal as they may seem, these little phrases are the folk wisdom of our age, the expression of a collective unconscious. These proverbs betray a fetishism of images. They can liberate by enabling us to become someone else, but they also have power over us because we need them to become what we want. What is revealed is an intense power we ascribe to images and a pressure we put on them: without them, we couldn't exist. What slips out is that for all the stories we might tell, words are not enough. Naming something is not enough to bring it into being. The self is not a speech act. Seeing is the way to the self, a river that can take us to who we want to be. But sight is also the medium of desire; desire is a current flowing through vision, propelling you of its own accord.

These pictures showed me the person I wanted to be. Since I needed them to show me that person, they knew more about him than I did. What else did they know?

In the years that followed, I went to every Tillmans exhibition I could. The small shows of new work that were regularly unveiled in his dealer's gallery in Bethnal Green in East London, the major retrospectives in Tate Britain. I bought editions of his early books: *Wolfgang Tillmans* (1995), *Burg* (1998), *truth study centre* (2005). I combed photographs of exhibition installations on his website and in catalogues. I wanted to know everything about this person, which no longer was Wolfgang Tillmans himself (nor, really, had it ever been), but the person I believed his pictures called into being. Who was he? What was I wanting in wanting to be him? What did he want?

After some time, I began to see one reason why he radiated a sense of belonging. Pictures of crowds at nightclubs and raves display the acceptance enabled by exclusion. You feel special, that you belong, because those who are a threat are kept out. The barriers to this world were not always as explicit as the doorman guarding the entry to a long queue of men waiting to enter Snax, a legendary sex and techno club in Berlin. They were often the more subtle walls raised up by celebrity and fame. From the mid-1990s, Tillmans' images begin to be populated by models like Kate Moss, DJs like Jeff Mills and Richie Hawtin, artists like Nan Goldin and Gilbert and George. As portraits in themselves, they are nothing special. They don't reveal some truth or insight about their subject. Instead, what is telling is the way these photographs are installed: arrayed on a gallery wall or laid out within the pages of a book. Photographs of the famous are displayed alongside those of the ordinary. Same format, same style, same world. There is no hierarchy, but it is unclear where this world of equality begins. Just beyond the bouncer or out here in the queue? What I wanted was to exclude as much as to belong.

This was the first friction I felt cutting against my desire to look like Wolfgang. The first nagging itch between desire and morality, a rash of worry as to whether they could be resolved. If I wanted to feel like I belong, to feel special, did that have to come at the cost of others being excluded? Do utopias need borders in order to be achieved?

Man pissing on a chair (1997). A skinny white man, wearing
nothing but black boots, blue jeans and red braces, is pissing
on a chair. His head is shaved, save for a short mohawk.
His bottom lip and his left nipple are pierced. In his right
hand, he holds a half-smoked cigarette; in his left, he holds
his penis, his thumb pulling back his foreskin. His target is
an office chair whose arms and legs are made from a single
Z-shaped metal tube and whose back and seat are made
from green fabric. The seat is soaked. Liquid drips onto the
wooden floor. Behind him stands a grey metal filing cabinet;
an office recedes into shadow. His milky body is illuminated
with light; his gaze is fixed on his piss; his self-absorption is
complete.

The skinhead was a look before it was an identity. It first
appeared in south and east London in the late 1960s. Its
defining elements – black or red boots, Levi's, braces and a
shaved head – were worn by white working-class teenagers
and Black migrants and their children, who had arrived in
London from Jamaica after the Second World War. The look
was a sign. It signalled a rejection of middle-class values,
pride in being working-class and an embrace of reggae and
ska. Jamaican producers soon coined a new musical genre to
match this new look: skinhead reggae. The look also began
to signify something else, at least from the publication of
Richard Allen's novel *Skinhead* (1970). Anger, rage, violence
and a virulent racism towards Black, Asian, and Jewish
people: anyone who wasn't white.

Ever since, the history of the skinhead has been the
history of a battle over what the look means. For some, the
skinhead is a subculture born from the interaction of Black
and white teenagers and the Empire that brought them

together. For others – fascist groups like the National Front, Blood and Honour and White Aryan Resistance – the look signalled white power, white pride and white hatred. When the skinhead appeared outside of Britain – when others began to want to look like a skinhead – the battle lines were blurred. In Germany and Eastern Europe, the skinhead was adopted by the neo-fascist groups that emerged, newly visible, after the fall of Communism, and its association with white racism was contested less by the Black inhabitants of those countries than their already existing antifascist groups whose members often also adopted the skinhead look. In Germany, the meaning of a skinhead was clear. In the year after the fall of the Berlin wall, racist attacks increased tenfold from 1990 to 1991. In 1992, hotels housing asylum seekers were burned to the ground by skinheads.

Gay skinheads have existed as long as the look itself, appearing in magazines like *The Young Londoners* in 1969. As with the early fetishisation of leather, this look enabled men who desired men to refute the assumption that to do so was feminising (as with his straight counterpart, the gay skinhead is running in fear away from femininity in those hard, heavy boots). And it enabled them to identify other men who shared that assumption (and that fear). To be a gay skinhead is to join a community of men who share a common desire to look like each other and to fuck one another. Yet, unlike other clones of masculinity – the lumberjack, the athlete, the jock – the skinhead look remained controversial after the politicisation of gay, lesbian and queer identities from the 1970s. In 1985, when, during a revival of the look in Britain, the first gay skinhead disco was organised at the London Gay Centre, lesbian members protested the event:

'By most people's standards, skinheads are fascists.' In his history of gay nightlife, Jeremy Atherton Lin encapsulates the complexities of the gay skinhead by telling the story of Nicky Crane. Crane was a ringleader in the far-right British Movement, leading gangs of skinheads to attack Black, Asian and Jewish Londoners in the 1980s. He was also a bouncer for the gay nightclub Heaven and eventually appeared in gay porn before renouncing both his fascism and his appearance. He died of AIDS in 1993.

It seems too simple to say that the gay attraction to the skinhead look is attraction to an image of masculinity since that begs the question: what is this masculinity? What is the sexuality that lies on the surface of these clothes? Jeans, leather boots, braces. These materials are thick, tough and functional. Their deployment requires care, control and pride. Boots need to be polished and laced, shirts to be ironed and buttoned. Their effect is violence and aggression. A boot hurts more than trainers; jeans protect more than tracksuits. All these meanings exist in opposition. To suits, sweatpants and sportswear. To dresses, skirts and heels. In each opposition, the skinhead occupies the dominating pole. To wear these clothes is to acquire these qualities, to be become proud, aggressive, in charge. To desire someone wearing these clothes is to want someone to take pride in violently dominating you as they shower you with acrid piss. The gay skinhead wants both at once, showing how entangled these two desires can be: to be something and to want to be fucked by something.

I soon began to see this entanglement in other images by Tillmans. Two photographs of a German soldier, taken from behind as he stands on a train. The thrill they give to the viewer of wondering whether the soldier knew and what he would do if you were caught. Four photographs, in series, showing a soldier with an AK47 entering a hotel room; the last one showing his gun and uniform on the floor beside his bare foot. A whole book called *Soldiers: The Nineties* (1999). I noticed something I missed the first time I looked, jealously, at the photograph of men queueing for the gay club, Snax. The bouncer was wearing military fatigues. And Tillmans himself, in the image I thought I wanted to become, was wearing combat pants. This eroticisation of military power was by no means a major theme in his work, just one among the infinite things that entered into his photographs. Yet, it was there, discomforting, jarring. Tillmans, these images, that bouncer. They were playing with these costumes of domination and violence. Yet, how could they be sure they could remain in control of what they meant? That someone wouldn't see a soldier as an object of fantasy, but as the man who kicked them out of their home, occupied their land, raped their mother? That blithe confidence Wolfgang had when wearing his army pants and boots.

More than a list of clothes, the skinhead is a look. It is something that can be made visible to others by specific clothes, a certain way of doing your hair. It is an appearance with meaning, and what that meaning is, is power. It promises that you can acquire power simply by looking powerful. That might be one reason for its origins and persistence among the working class: power, by definition, is what they do not have. And that promise is premised on the power of looking: that we can control how others see us. This is why I came to think, after years staring at that piss, that the skinhead has been so sought after by adherents of whiteness, even as it remains used by others. Whiteness is, above all, a system for deploying power: who rules, who suffers, who lives, who dies. It does so in a myriad of ways – law, language, the concentration of toxins in water – yet, its one foundational mechanism is appearance: what human bodies look like. Whiteness wants difference to be visible, hence its need to create one-drop rules and impose yellow stars if that visibility gets threatened. White power wants to control by controlling the meaning of what bodies look like. Whiteness, among many things, is control. It is the power to decide what bodies look like. Whiteness is the desire *that* bodies look like.

'I want to fuck a skinhead / hard / ripping flesh / thrust all twelve inches of black / down his sewered hole . . . I'm gonna pump history darker with every stroke.' Sabah As-Sabah's poem, 'Invocation', shows one kind of pleasure Black men can take from fucking with the skinhead: dominating and possessing that which has dominated you. But when white gay men both desire and desire to be a skinhead, they fuck with sharing the power of whiteness as much as they subvert it. This is not just the specific powers of violence, aggression and pride but the power to play with images of power, the power to enjoy images of violence and being images of violence. And the power to play comes from possessing the power to decide what bodies look like. That is the power that fucks with them, whether they like it or not.

I've never wanted to look like a skinhead. Or a soldier, a policeman or a thug. Nor have I ever found them especially attractive. (I mean, I would, but in spite of.) The reason might be as simple as the fact that I am not a member of the urban working class. But that seems too easy. The skinhead as a look attracts gay men across classes, ethnicities, racially classified bodies. It's not about identity; it's about erotics. So, what it is then? If it's not about who someone is on the inside, but about the texture of what lies on the surface, what didn't I want to wear or to touch? I didn't want boots laced tight; I wanted things I could easily prise open. I didn't want thick, rough jeans; I wanted revealing, clinging cotton. I didn't want stubble; I wanted silk. I didn't want hard; I wanted soft.

Softness isn't the absence of power. There is more control in a caress than in a blow. More strength in holding than hitting. More permanence in a delicate embrace than in a stain of piss. Softness is as much a kink as anything. Dominance and submission create the pressure that makes desire flow; I knew this was as true for me as it was for anyone. That this pressure could be just as powerful when tender, that it could be applied with more force by a lazy stroke than a stomping boot. Maybe that was my utopia.

Fantastic Man 11. A portrait of Wolfgang Tillmans appears on the cover of *Fantastic Man* magazine in 2010. He is holding a white phone with a curling cord to his ear with his left hand; he is holding a mug in his right. The back and sides of his head are shaved; the top is thicker, demarcated by a clear line. His blue eyes seem sad, like he is receiving some troubling news. He is wearing a white t-shirt, red braces and faded denim jeans. The photo is cropped just below his crotch, but I knew if my gaze could travel down his leg, I would see heavy black boots pressing down on the side of my bloody, crying face.

I had never wanted to look like a skinhead. Yet, I had

wanted to look like Wolfgang, who had wanted to look like a skinhead. I had stepped into a hall of mirrors, filled with fog and illuminated with low neon lights, where each reflection showed what its viewer wanted to be. Tillmans: a skinhead, a powerful man, a soldier, a Nazi. But also, around a corner: an artist, a success, the subject of a portrait. And another: a beloved, a lover, an obsession, a friend.

I had wanted a mirror, not a maze. I had wanted to look like someone else in order to become who I wanted to be. I had wanted someone else to show me who I desired to be, showing that, like all desire, our greatest fantasy is that someone else knows what we want before we do, that we never have to even ask. More than this – I had been seduced by the idea that what I looked like revealed who I was. And I had believed, in the cloud of desire, that what he looked like was the truth of who he was. I wanted our bodies to look like something. I wanted to be able to decide what bodies looked like and, until I saw the image of the person I wanted to be as a skinhead, I never doubted I had that power. Wolfgang Tillmans taught me who I wanted to be, that this wasn't who I was or who I ever might become. He also taught me something of what it means to be white. That I, too, wanted to control what bodies looked like. I, too, wanted that power.

* * *

Freischwimmer 190 (2011). The image is large. It is higher and wider than I am tall. I could fit inside it, stretching out my arms. It is blue, a field of lighter and darker shades merging in and out of one another. Thin black lines emerge from these gradations of navy and cornflower, tracing patterns across its surface. A comb of lines arches from left to right, culminating in a scatter of pinpricks. Down the middle, these lines converge into a dark zigzag that vertically bisects the pools of blue. It looks, of all things, like the contours of the ridge that rises beneath the Atlantic Ocean, in a line midway between Africa and the Americas, underwater mountains formed by the force that drives continents apart. What you see looks like it was taken underwater, the dappled light formed by ripples on a surface, the lines the blur of eyelashes as you squint to see in an unfamiliar world. But we are always finding likenesses where none are intended to exist.

Around 1998, Tillmans began making what he called his abstract pictures. There were photographs made without using a camera or lens. For his *Silver* series, he ran photosensitive paper through a copier and then exposed it to light, revealing the specks of dirt it had picked up. For the *Freischwimmer* series, he exposed photographic paper to handheld light sources, producing modulations of line and light across single fields of colour. Tillmans began making these pictures at a time when he began to feel the world was 'over-photographed'. His career as a photographer corresponds, almost exactly, with the emergence of mass digital photography, mobile phones and the internet; the JPEG, the World Wide Web and the iPhone. These technologies, whose infrastructures would soon appear in his photographs, have transformed the world of images; their algorithms, which can create images from images, have made it a self-replicating infinity. These abstract photographs might seem to be a refusal of the digital transformation of photography. They are created by chemicals and paper, not data and pixels. They take analogue photography back to its essence as an index of reality, a physical trace of the world. They also might seem to be a failure, or a loss of faith, in Tillman's desire to see the world photographed. They don't try to make a likeness of the visible world; they are an object in that world. Yet, no less than any of his images, these pictures are the outcome of a relation. One thing depends on another; one thing brings another into being. Chemicals and paper; dirt and light.

In 2005, Tillmans embarked on another strand of work that took him further away from ravers and skinheads, fruit and water. The *Truth Study Centre* manifested less in a particular genre of photography than on tables: the long vitrines I had encountered at the first exhibition of his work that I saw. These were his 'truth study tables': photocopies of magazines and printouts of websites documenting an increasing disagreement about things that, to Tillmans, once seemed self-evident. Whether AIDS was caused by HIV. Whether women should determine what happens to their own bodies. Whether vaccines worked. And later, after the financial crisis of 2008 and the election of Donald Trump and Britain's vote to leave the European Union (both in 2016), whether democracy worked. Whether capitalism worked. Whether even if the truth was something one could achieve with certainty. Whether truth is what people still wanted. This study of truth is prescient and also poignant, the long documentation of disillusion. It is the recognition that the work is full of difference, not similarity. And this is not the difference of a relaxed cosmopolitanism, that globalised world where Tillmans can photograph people in

Hong Kong, Addis Ababa or Sao Paolo. This was the kind of difference where people don't even see the same thing. Tillmans never frames his photographs, but these studies of truth are placed under glass on tables. As if the truth was more fragile than any image.

17 Years Supply (2014). The photograph is taken from above, looking down over a rectangular cardboard box full of empty medicine bottles. The edges of the picture closely frame the sides of the box so that you can only see a surface of white containers framed by brown cardboard. It is too close to see how deep the box is. The labels are addressed to Wolfgang Tillmans and show the names of the pharmacies in London that dispensed these prescriptions. The labels contain instructions: 'Take two capsules with or after food, once each day'. On one bottle, guidance is written by hand in black marker: 'Keep in . . .' The drugs have names like Epivir, Norvir, Reyataz, Truvada and Videx EC. They are the medicines that have kept Tillmans alive ever since he was diagnosed with HIV, 17 years before the photograph was taken. They have been doing so ever since, a whole life built on a jumble of plastic and paper.

I first saw this photograph in 2019 in an exhibition in Dublin, the city where I first had sex, which is to say, the city where I first thought I would contract HIV and die of AIDS. The exhibition was held in a building originally constructed in the 17th century as a military hospital. The long narrow exhibition galleries, flanking a central courtyard, retained the memory of their past use as wards for the sick as they displayed images of fragility: a breaking wave, broken eggshells, a patient undergoing open-heart surgery. The exhibition gathered photographs largely from the years between 2009 and 2019, and they showed a very different world from that that I first imagined his work offered, when I was seduced – when I needed to be seduced – five years earlier. Here were images onto which I couldn't project my desire of likeness but which served as a reminder of difference. A photograph of a protest from 2006 showed a banner proclaiming: 'Nice Here But Ever Been To Kyrgyzstan? Free Gender Expression Worldwide'. Another showed a portrait of a sexual health clinic in Kakuma Refugee Camp in Kenya, alongside a book documenting Tillmans' years of campaigning for better access to HIV medicine for people in Africa. A book from 2015 asked, *What's Wrong with Redistribution?* Its title served as a reminder of everything I had that others had not. It also served as a challenge to the belief that I was, in fact, seeing images of difference. In what way, other than mere appearance, was anyone in these photographs not like me?

But this I now knew: there was nothing mere about appearance. To look and to look like were the means I used to create a self. And if creation aims to produce something that never existed, this looking led away from that which produced it: the absence of any sense of self in the first place. To look like Wolfgang was a means to an end, yet that end was as much an identity as it was the object of a desire. To want to look like someone made it impossible to untangle whose desire was whose: mine, his, an anonymous crowd of others. This might be the outcome of the strange form of desire that wants a body that is both the same and different, that is, wanting to have it both ways: wanting too much. Or it might just be the impossibility of ever figuring out who decided who we wanted to be.

It could have been those boys, softly entangled in

Arcadia, lying in shorts on a sofa, grinning on a kitchen sink. The desire for a look, a self, an identity: this is to want to be someone who belongs, someone soft enough to be held by another. It's the desire for love that shows the difference between love and desire, for if to love is to accept things as they are, to desire is that which will get you there. Or it could have been the skinhead, forever pissing on a chair, who wants, and wants to be, something solid and hard enough to transgress, to shame, of which to be ashamed, to debase, to place under taboo, to crush beneath the hard edge of a boot. It could have been the desire for power and for control.

It is because they both involve the deployment of power that desire and politics can sometimes feel so inextricable. You can't just confine sex to the bedroom, or the club, and politics to the ballot box, or to what comes out of the barrel of a gun. It is politics that decides who has a bedroom; it is desire that gives force to the look of that gun. Perhaps they are more fundamentally entangled because both contest the terrain of identity. Desire involves wanting to be someone as much as wanting to have something. Politics involves deciding who 'we' are: who is in and who is out. My desire to look like Wolfgang was a desire for the power to belong to an entire world, but that wasn't the same kind of power that could bring that world into being. Looking like someone can create a self, but it can't build a world for others to inhabit. Likeness can be the basis for desire, but it is not enough for politics.

At first, I thought the genre I was seeking for my story was comedy, one that would end in the resolution of the conflict between desire and politics, a happy ending that discovered both could be united in a glorious utopia, free of the operation of power, where all I needed was love. Ten years later, at that final exhibition, I thought it might be tragedy, whose ending was the realisation that the clash between desire and politics was an unavoidable fate. But now I realised it was both, a tragicomic tale of the self, since if our likenesses are who we want to be, then life is just an autobiography of attachments. The desire for likeness as a means to belong requires a disavowal of likeness to bring a world of belonging into being. Wanting to have it both ways – well, that is one form of preparation for having neither. What else is there to do but laugh at the impossibility of what you want?

Tillmans' uncertainty about what had happened to the future he once envisaged was shown in a display of texts on a wall from a work called *Time Mirrored*: '1969 was 24 years from 1945. Twenty-four years back from now is 1994. Martin Luther King Jr's 'I Have a Dream' speech was 27 years prior to 1990. Twenty-seven years past 1990, Donald J. Trump was sworn in as president of the United States.' These little statements, facts ventriloquising confusion, have appeared throughout his work, in books, exhibitions and magazines. What does the passing of years mean? Is time past the same as time future? Does time have a direction: forwards, backwards, up, down? For all their confusion, they do show a faith in chance correspondences. Or maybe just a willingness to ascribe them, so meaningless in themselves, with all the power of a fate written in the stars.

Hale-Bopp (1997). The photograph is small, about the size of the palm of my hand. It shows a sky at dusk, blue ceding to black and a wash of neon pink clouds. In the middle of the sky, a comet burns white, tracing a path of light in its wake.

1997 is ten years after 1987. The Hale-Bopp comet was only first discovered in 1995, and when it appeared in the sky, it introduced something wholly new to the world, something that had never been seen before. When I saw it in one of Tillmans' books, it appeared, as if by chance, on the page before the picture of the skinhead. I spent so long looking at the skinhead it took me a long time to notice the small caption at the bottom of the page, identifying the name of the comet. It was the first thing in over a decade of looking at Tillmans' work that I had seen with my own eyes. I had finally looked like Wolfgang.

DANCING ON OUR OWN

1. *John Maus – Do Your Best*

> *'Someone / Someone's alone / In the city / Tonight'*

We had been waiting. Waiting was one of the few things we could do. Time was something we had in excess. We had the time to set up our laptops on our desks, or kitchen tables, or chairs, so we could have room to move – not that one person dancing on their own needs much room. We had time to connect our computers to our speakers, to set up the live stream on our phones and the video call on our laptops so we could see each other better and the sounds wouldn't echo and lag. Sarah and Oonagh ended up explaining how to make it all work. Luke and Hannah were sitting down to dinner. Tom had projected their screen onto a wall, so when we looked at them, we saw ourselves in a grid of light, drinking, each in our own rooms in our own homes, waiting for Robyn to join us.

*'Reach out your hands to the one alone | In your
city tonight'*

Robyn's greatest gift as a singer is to fulfil the double-sided
promise of pop music: that no one's feelings are so unique
that they can't be given expression in someone else's song and
that by giving up belief in your own individuality, you will
gain the consolation of belonging. No one's experience is so
exceptional that someone else can't compose its soundtrack,
and Robyn had written the score for our nights out and walks
home, our sex and our breakups, our morning cycles across
London Bridge and our long nights together in bed, just like
she was now providing the soundtrack to the film our lives
had become, as we lived them, together, on our screens.

'Someone | Someone's alone | In your city'

Like all pop stars, Robyn offers herself as an image onto
which we can project our dreams and desires, including,
that night, the collective fantasy that she – our favourite –
had decided to play a DJ set live online on a Friday night in
April 2020, just for us, because we needed it. Forbidden from
dancing together, unable to touch one another, confined in
our separate rooms, living alone for the first time: of course,
she knew we needed this; of course, someone cared. As she
appeared on screen behind turntables and speakers in the
corner of a mirrored room, her image refracted into an infinity
of mirrored rooms. Of course, she had kept her promise,
opening with a slow hymn in synth, whose lyrics, repeating
over and over again, suddenly made our world so simple.

'Someone | Someone's alone | In your city | Tonight'

2. *Prince – I Wish U Heaven*

Robyn was no more playing her set for us than she was playing it for the hundreds of other people whose comments began appearing below the video, everyone expressing the same joy. But that didn't matter; that has never mattered. So many of my earliest attachments to music were born out of these kinds of misrecognitions. To believe it is self-evident that a song has the meaning we want it to have or the singer the intent that matches our own, only to discover, much later, that none of it was true. And to discover this doesn't matter, that the intensity of those first moments of music describing our reality isn't dimmed by the revelation that it was all just a fantasy.

Oh, my mistakes were legion. I thought that when Lou Reed was waiting for his man, he was waiting for his boyfriend, not his heroin dealer. I thought that when Dee Dee Ramone was waiting on the corner of 53rd and 3rd in Manhattan, he was hoping to meet a lover, not sell himself as a hustler. When I tried to imitate the confidence of Debbie Harry as she sang about her dreaming, I thought I was imitating the confidence of a young and beautiful punk, not the cynicism of a woman in her 30s who has seen too much to believe in dreams anymore. And when I first heard Prince, as a teenager growing up in the country, taking a bus journey once a week to the next town over in order to buy CDs: then, as now, I was sure that someone like that was wishing heaven to someone like me.

These kinds of misrecognitions, the kind that, unlike affairs of the flesh, survive their contact with reality, could only have happened to someone who was alone. Someone who had no friends who listened to the same kind of music, friends whose knowledge could quickly, and brutally, clarify any mistakes of interpretation, or whose own fantasies would quickly smother any competition. They could only happen to someone who didn't yet have the internet, or at least who wasn't allowed to spend hours on it late at night, trawling through message boards, decoding the meaning hidden in every songs' lyrics. They could only have happened, that is, to someone who wasn't who we were now.

These kinds of misrecognitions are born from a loneliness so strong that even when you discover that Prince's desire only curls around men as an afterthought, if at all; that the very sense of Prince being excessively sexual says nothing about him and everything about what I was taught to believe sex should be; that even when you make the mistake of watching *Purple Rain* the film and seeing the contempt Prince can perform for women; even after all this, the laceration left by encountering the reality of his desire was never so fatal that the wound didn't heal, and a purple scar didn't form as a memorial to the dream that had been damaged, but not destroyed. That Prince, then and now, like all the objects of our desire, really does wish us heaven.

3. *Choker – Gradient*

Nostalgia and novelty are the two charged poles electrifying a DJ set. The simple fact that so much music is first heard alone in those years before you can go out, before you can hear it with others, means that those first intense fusions with a song belong in the past. Hearing that music again in a crowd, sounding differently when played by a band on stage or emerging from the dance-floor fog like an old lover, always brings us back to the moments when we first heard it alone.

But nostalgia is also a kind of death, suffocating the development of a sound, calcifying it in stone. Northern soul was born when working-class teenagers in England's industrial towns decided that the canon of Black American soul was complete. No new songs could be allowed to be played; no new fashions or dances could be introduced, and a fear of loss has preserved their frenzy of love in amber ever since. Nostalgia for music denies that anything new can ever happen to us, that things will occur that need new soundtracks, new movements. None of us ever imagined we would never be able to go out again. Not to Corsica, not to the Vaults, not to Bethnal Green Working Men's Club, not the George. Nor that afterwards we could never again pile back to someone's house and wind down together. Yet, there we were, two drinks in, learning what this sounded like.

None of us knew the third song, but to let each other know, we had to stop dancing and type on our laptops. Mine was on my desk, against one long wall of the rectangular main room in my flat, kitchen at one end, balcony at the other. My kitchen table and sofa were pushed back against the wall to give me room to dance. I was drinking cheap white wine in a plastic cup, trying to recreate some sense of normalcy. I was wearing a vest, sports shorts and trainers. If it was going to be different, at least I would be comfortable, and I would have one night where I didn't ruin my good clothes with sweat. Even with so little on, I was warming up.

4. *Raze – Break 4 Love*

Blondie and The Ramones, Prince and The Velvet Underground. Like so many boys with aspirations, with notions of tragic isolation, these were the sounds of my teenage years. It was music that never fully devoted itself to the sole task of making you dance, though I treasured the moments when it came close, like on the shimmering seven-inch remix of 'Heart of Glass' that I had on my deluxe album edition, a glittery curtain that seemed to open to another, unknown world. That world wasn't the dance music I knew. 'Dance music' to me, at the beginning of the new millennium, was hard, glossy, repellent – the equivalent in sound of the mirrored covers of Ministry of Sound mix CDs or the tanned bodies on Ibiza Uncovered, a television show where lads and their girls fucked and vomited to fast metallic trance. It was the music of hard cunts from town who held raves out the country, dealers who had cars, who took pills and fought while their girlfriends looked on. It was music that didn't ask to be touched. Where could you move in that?

When I moved to Dublin to go to university, it was by accident that I first heard a different kind of dance music. At two in the morning, drunken students will go anywhere that will take them. We went to the basements of pubs and the counters of shiny bars playing the pop music we already knew. And sometimes we ended up in the last club open, playing music that was different, music I didn't want to get drunk to, music whose loops and textures were deep and rich, a web that would hold me in time. I hadn't the nerve to ask anyone to come with me, too insecure to realise they needed something to hold them too, so I started going out on my own, to nights whose flyers advertised 'house / techno / electro', nights with names like Nightflight, Backlash and Family. And I wouldn't really drink; I would just go right up to the speakers on my own and lose myself and dance.

And then, invited back to houses to continue into the next day, I would learn. In the slower tempo that came with morning, the music would go back in time, back to the funk and disco out of which dance music was born, catalysed by technology: turntables, sound systems, 12-inch records, drum machines. I learned that house music was Black and gay and invited you in if you weren't, an openness that threatened its undoing. And that people like Larry Heard and Nicky Siano were still alive and still DJing and would come to play small clubs in Dublin, and that their descendants, like Levon Vincent and Omar-S, would come and play even smaller pub basements in Ireland, forgotten by the America that was their home.

I learned that Vaughan Mason was a music producer from Chicago who began his career managing soul singers before forming a short-lived band, Vaughan Mason and Crew, whose 'Boogie, Skate, Rock and Roll,' from 1980, was sampled in everything from hip-hop to French house, by A Tribe Called Quest and by Daft Punk. I learned that in the late 80s, he produced 'Break 4 Love' as Raze, spacing out the rhythms of soul, funk and disco with drum machines and synthesisers, in a transformation that encapsulated how so much house music was born.

Whole histories can get summoned up by a single song. That night, the drop that opens 'Break 4 Love' was taking part in another history. In the song's break, its invitation to love is met by clips of a woman's voice breathing, panting, screaming on the border between pain and pleasure, cut and repeated to become just another rhythm accompanying the bass, gasping like someone about to come or someone whose lungs are being pumped by a ventilator.

Whole lives can lie hidden behind a single song. The lives of so many producers of early dance music can remain unknown to those listening to them far away across time and place. A couple of weeks before we danced, Vaughan Mason died at the age of 69. I later found a post on a message board online that said his death was caused by Covid-19.

5. *Chez Damier – A1 Untitled*

In the beginning, 'house' wasn't a specific genre of music. It didn't have any single defining feature; it didn't have a distinct identity as a sound. It was simply music played at The Warehouse, a club that opened in Chicago in 1977 by Frankie Knuckles. Soul, funk, disco, gospel, electronic European pop – whatever made its members-only clientele of Black and Latino gay men dance. Knuckles and his best friend Larry Levan grew up in the Bronx and established themselves as DJs playing in The Continental Baths, a gay bathhouse with a nightclub, restaurant and apartments. This was music for sex and what came afterwards. When Levan left the Baths to open the Paradise Garage, the club that brought disco to perfection, Knuckles moved to Chicago to set up a club of his own and, free from the whims of fashion that were so dangerous in New York, Knuckles transformed disco, long after it was declared dead, into something new. House, he once said, was disco's revenge.

Revenge took the form of extending songs by playing them back-to-back on two turntables or editing them on reel-to-reel tape machines, doubling breakdowns, stripping out verses, adding beats. It aimed to make music that simply went 'On & On', as Jesse Saunders named a record from 1984 in which you can hear disco breaking down into its component parts and becoming something new. Radio DJs like Farley Keith Williams began to add the synthetic kick-drum beat of a 909 drum machine to these remixed records and then to use drum machines to make rhythm tracks of their own. And after these records were played in The Warehouse to young dancers like Chez Damier, they were remixed again into tracks that were leaner, faster, purely about movement.

Almost as soon as it had a name, house music couldn't stop naming itself. Songs identified themselves with the power of a name: house. And not long after it had a name, records began to tell the story of its creation, most famously, in Rhythm Control's 'My House' (1987): 'In the beginning, there was jack, and jack had a groove, and from this groove came the groove of all grooves / And while one day viciously throwing down on his box, jack declared let there be house, and house music was born.'

Dance music can't be defined, but if one had to compile a list of its features, it would include: music that raises its origins to the level of myth. The true sound was born in worlds now long departed; the best clubs are those that are now closed; the greatest nights are those that no longer take place. Perhaps these myths need to be made in service of memory since, like so much music created by Black Americans, the world outside was interested in selling the music but not remembering the people who made it. Perhaps the reason dance music is so haunted with the fear of being forgotten is because it is a music that doesn't exist for itself but for a purpose: to make people dance. And people grow up and stop going out and different people take their place and crowds change and what will make them dance will change. Perhaps because the music is always changing, it always needs to look back, always to create its myths.

Myths need believers; it's only while someone has faith that they continue to exist. These myths have always drawn me to music, and I've always been the most credulous believer, accepting what may be the greatest myth of all: that the history of something so complex as house music can have a single story. I've always known that when I felt at home in house music, I was believing in a myth. The closer I got towards it, the more I memorised names and dates and label numbers, the further it moved away. The more I learned of its origins in Chicago, New York and New Jersey, the more I realised how little about those origins I would ever know.

6. *Kevin Over – Basic Cut*

I once flew to Kiev on my own for the sole purpose of going out – in the morning – to a club called Closer. I rented a flat in a refurbished Soviet apartment block, no doubt the intended clientele. During the day, I bought plums and cherries outside the decaying modernist fruit market, a swooping roof of concrete rising to a future that never arrived. At dawn, I woke up and walked out of the city towards the hills where yellowing walls gave way to abandoned buildings from the

19ᵗʰ century: grain silos, warehouses and train sheds. In a
factory, painted red, I went upstairs to a room that shut out
the day. Inside, the music was hard, very hard, the kind of
techno that hurts.

Dancing alone allows you to enter yourself, but it also
allows you to observe others, together but not belonging.
The crowd was young, uniformly pale and thin, wearing
military gear, perhaps in sympathy with those fighting in
the war with Russia in the east of the country. And over
their military fatigues, they wore another set of symbols
recognised the world over: rainbows, pink ribbons, AIDS
badges. After a while, I moved outside to a wooden patio
surrounded by raised platforms among a forest of trees
whose branches were rigged with sprinklers that released a
mist onto the bodies below. This crowd was older, pale from
dancing inside all night, men in football shirts, women in
bikinis, and yet, the softer morning music wasn't inspiring
anyone to touch.

Here is another myth, born like all great myths, from
a kernel of truth. Techno was born when three Black
teenagers from Detroit – Juan Atkins, Derrick May and
Kevin Saunderson – were captivated by the music they
heard when they went out in Chicago but wanted to
make that music at home. Their sensibility was different.
Machines, rather than human flesh; the technology of
the future, not the parties of the past. At home, in their
bedrooms, they used drum machines and production
equipment to create their own synthetic sounds from
scratch, rather than sample the vocals and instrumentals
on tracks that already existed. Ignored in America, their
music was lionised in Europe and, when interviewed by a

group of British music journalists, Atkins named it techno. Techno found its second home in Europe in the ruins left behind by that continent's propensity to self-annihilation. After the fall of the Berlin Wall, it echoed in the rubble of a city half-destroyed by war and occupation. After the destruction of the welfare state, the reward for the same war that ruined Berlin, its numbing pounding beats gave solace to the north of England, where it was speeded up, made into acid, exported to Ibiza and then, to the world.

You hear these myths replayed over and over again in records made decades later. In Kevin Over's 'Basic Cut', you hear two vocal samples looping out of the acoustic space in which we were losing ourselves. 'Chicago in here' – a song made by someone born in Germany's Ruhr Valley, tracing its origins back to a club that opened over ten years before he was born. 'This is what we eat, sleep and breathe' – the anthem of all those who live for that tradition of going out, losing oneself, recovering and repeating it over and over again in a life as repetitive as the music that gives it form.

The crowd promises a kind of unity in its anonymity. Here, we are all equal; here, we just want to forget who we are and be nothing more than people who love the same sounds. But the crowd is not free of the divisions it pretends to hold at bay: who gets paid and who earns nothing; who gets to touch and who is made ashamed; who gets remembered and who gets forgotten. That the crowd keeps making that promise in spite of it all – its greatest gift or its deepest deception?

7. *Robyn – Honey (Avalon Emerson's Deep Current Reroll)*

It feels like the same thing over and over again.

It feels like returning to the same thing over and over again is the way to make things change.

It feels like repetition is insistence.

It feels like insistence is paying attention.

It feels like taking off your jacket, taking off your top, stripping down to shorts and a t-shirt and just going for it.

It feels like your heartbeat becomes the world.

It feels like being hit, only without the pain.

It feels like submission.

It feels like willed submission.

It feels like you are moving under someone else's orders, that you will hear something as long as someone else wants you to hear it, that if when you get tired you can't sit down, that the choice to stop is not your own.

It feels like a question: why would you want this to end?

It feels like, at some point, things shift gears.

That you don't know what time it is, but you have never been more aware of time's passing.

That you don't even want to play the game of eyeing someone up and waiting for them to look back, to spend a song slowly moving through the crowd towards them, waiting to see who will be the first to risk a touch.

That it's always best when you have space, to dance, to be with air.

That it's always best at dawn.

That you don't need to speak to people to know them.

That you don't need to know people to belong.

That the feeling things have shifted is the thing you keep going back for.

It feels like you will spend the rest of your life going back for it, but that you will never find it.

It feels like a cramp in your thighs – the thighs are always the first to go.

It feels like bursting outside for air and inhaling nothing but smoke.

It feels like the answer to the titles of all those songs: Can You Feel It, Can You Feel The Bass, House (Is A Feeling), Jack Is The Feeling, I Feel Love.

It feels like being stuck in the sweetest, thickest thing.

It feels like honey.

8. *Oni Ayhun – OAR003-B*

This one Sarah already knew. Somehow the knowledge in her smile, visible even across a blurry screen, was enough to set us off. We let go into a simple four to the floor, then an even simpler high-hat 16 beat, then that rare but delicious thing: a melody emerging from the speakers like a face from the crowd, short enough to be memorised at the beginning and to be anticipated all the way to the end.

We let go into the drop of a beat falling across the melody, the back and forth between beat and tune creating the boundaries of a space in which to bounce side to side, and we trailed our hands to the rise and fall of strings. We interpreted the music for one another, we caught a glimpse of each other's eyes across our screens, and we couldn't believe how happy we were.

Tom had started the song in pink leather shorts, but after the first breakdown, they reappeared in a flowing navy dress, holding a yellow sheet in their hand, and they traced shapes with fabric across their screen, and then they changed again, into a white vest and those pink shorts. And I thought that this is why I love them, their capacity to change, their courage in doing so, something I found so hard, and how friendship is never wanting someone to be anything other than what they already are.

I saw Sarah and Oonagh immersed in one another when they appeared on screen, since they were falling into the dark like they had fallen into each other. I remembered how they had first met in a queue for a club, how Sarah was going in and Oonagh was leaving to go home, only to turn around and go back in again. I thought about how Sarah melted into our group of friends. I thought about how Oonagh had always taken care of me but refused to be a surrogate mother and how friendship is knowing exactly what someone thinks they want and knowing the right way not to give it to them.

I saw Luke and Hannah dancing, finally, properly for the first time, in that house where we all knew we had a room if we needed it, even now, when that wasn't allowed. I thought of how friendship can maintain itself across silence, without being with someone for a long time, since sometimes all you need to know is that someone will be there, in the dark, even when you can't see them.

It all hit like a wave, like a rush of someone else's euphoria, which maybe is the only way happiness can hit us, from outside. That might lie at the root of the suspicion of it all: the music, the manufactured feelings, the synthetic joy. As if the only things that are valuable are things you create on your own. As if you should ever be able to do this on your own.

9. *Erasure – Always*

For all my obsession with the history of house and techno, all the poring through record catalogues, all the fantasies I spun about DJs and their lives, I've never been a purist, which is to say, I've always been a fraud. I've never been one of those who I've thought are really committed. Those who, on their nights out, demand only to hear their sound, the sound they can't hear elsewhere. Those competing as they stand on the sides of a dancefloor to identify a track or a mix – though I've never understood, as I watched them nod their heads, how they inform everyone else of their victory, across the noise of the music they compete to know.

I treasure any passion that requires prohibitions; I would defend it to the death. But I've never been one for whom it is taboo to disrupt electronic soundscapes and looping rhythms with the particular, sweating, singing voice. I've never been able to wholly commit to the coolness that, far from repressing feeling, instead dissipates it into vibrating floors and sweat-stained walls. For I've never been able to resist that moment, after dawn, when the mix cuts, and you are all invited to sing.

Erasure's 'Always' is a song that takes the drama of its emotions so seriously, so absent of irony, that it feels like an affront. Like so many synth-pop ballads from the 80s that grew out of early electronic music and seem ludicrous now, they entice with their licence to enter those realms of feeling dismissed as hysterical, theatrical, excessive. Bronski Beat's 'Small Town Boy', Ultravox's 'Vienna', everything by Alison Moyet. They are songs that pull you out of hours of entranced isolation and onto an imaginary stage, everyone in the crowd becoming your audience while simultaneously demanding you become their audience as we sing together to Whitney, Madonna, Cher. And of course, Robyn, who has spent her career creating those songs in which the façade drops, the pretence of appearing desirable dissolves, and you all become, for one long messy song, friends.

Every night has one of these songs; often, the same song gets played for the same crowd, the song that gets played just before the end. On tiny balconies and in packed kitchens, I learned by heart the lyrics of 'Never Too Much' by Luther Vandross and 'Together in Electric Dreams' by Philip Oakey. I've been a guest in crowds for whom it all ends, walking down the street, with 'To Be Real' by Cheryl Lynn. These are songs that offer the overperformance of theatricality and melodrama so that even if they only pull us some of the way, they allow us the permission of the performer: the pretence that we are someone else singing the words singing we want to say; that it is Erasure, and not us, crying: Hold on, to the night, there will be no shame . . .

There has always been something strange about these songs – they can only happen once in a night. Played too much, the sentiment they allow comes to feel fake, unearned, cheap. These anthems are a testimony to how joy is as complicated as any serious emotion. Its value comes from its rarity. And yet that rarity doesn't reduce the experience of joy to fleeting, evanescent moments. We feel it as much in its anticipation as its recollection – maybe even more. Just like being with our friends, we wouldn't want it all of the time since that would mean forgoing holding it in memory, which is just another way of hoping it might come again.

10. *Lime – Babe, We're Gonna Love Tonight*

There is an intensity that people can emanate on a night out like an aura that surrounds them as they dance and sing to themselves, an intensity that comes from an intention to use the night to let go. You enter the long hours between midnight and dawn knowing what you need to expel, knowing what you are clinging to, and in the dark, you decide to let go. But there are times when music forces you to let go, where the release isn't planned and, for all those reasons, is more intense. Perhaps that is what we were chasing all those years, and again, dancing with each other, on our screens.

A seven-pulse blast of a synthesised horn snaps us out of our operatic melodramas. It repeats over and over again, joined by a simple melody played with chimes and a beat just on the edge of frantic. It's a song I've never heard before, but as it loops over and over again, like a fire alarm left to ring, a giddy high leaves me bouncing, spinning, as if dancing to a siren announcing the end of the world.

Lime was a couple from Montréal who started to release disco records in 1979: Denyse LePage and her partner, who then recorded under the name of Denis LePage but who since then transitioned and is, today, Nini Nobless. Their songs are simple to the point of being crude and all the better for it; Nini singing then in a growling baritone, Denyse in a barely-functioning falsetto. In their videos, they sway in satin shirts and silk robes, blurred and coloured by cheap televisual effects, looking and sounding like a straight suburban couple suddenly bursting their bounds. As they squeal and howl that they are going to love tonight, pulsing with the urge of abandon, you feel just how much energy disco music threatened to release once it left Black and gay clubs and bathhouses and seeped into bedrooms all around the world. The looping siren that anchors the entire song begins to sound like the warning of a coming nuclear meltdown. As if, when a siren sounded disaster, you chose not to flee but to dance to it.

Thursday, July 12, 1979, was Disco Demolition Night. At the end of a game organised by Major League Baseball in Comiskey Park, Chicago, a crate of disco records was blown up by explosives in front of a braying crowd of tens of thousands. That year, rock fans, mostly white men, had crusaded across American radio announcing that 'Disco Sucks', destroying stacks of records with chainsaws, demanding, in the words of one instigating DJ Robert Dahl, the 'eradication of the dreaded musical disease known as DISCO'. They did it not because they heard disco played by DJs like Larry Levan or Nicky Siano, who were Black or gay, and everything that entailed in their minds. They did it because they heard records by bands like Lime, by couples who looked just like them, and they just knew what they threatened.

In the second half of 1979, thousands of clubs closed in the United States alone, and disco disappeared back into the underground from where it first emerged, only to ferment and concentrate, like wine distilling into spirits, into the sound that Lime begins to touch, the sound known as Hi-NRG. Hi-NRG is disco but faster, harder, its sounds more artificial and astringent. It was the sound of a different disease emerging in gay clubs as AIDS began to empty their dancefloors. It is the sound of dancing in desperation; its frantic tempo, beyond the range of sober movement, is the sound of time running out, a sound that says if you want to let go, you better hurry up, for there soon won't be any time left.

11. *Prince – Purple Music*

You're always already there when you discover you've gone too far. When you've been out too long, dancing too much. When you've lost your friends and lost yourself.

The song frustrated me at first. We had been so deep in it; we had been coming together through music we had never even heard before; we had been hitting that feeling even tonight, in this desperate attempt to replicate a happiness we could no longer pursue and, for a while, I believed we had. Then this stuttering down-tempo bassline and a wandering discordant melody that had the shape of deciding you can't come because you are too wasted.

Luke and Hannah had disappeared; Tom was just walking around, not replying to messages. I was wet and sat down to drink some water. Prince was playing again as if to mark how far we had come, that it had been an hour, the realisation that it has been an hour a downer, like the lights coming on to reveal everything we had mutually agreed not to see. Even when they go back out again, something of the complicit fantasy never returns.

I thought I may as well get a little drunk since everyone else was flagging. 'Purple Music' is a song about flagging, ten minutes of tight, closed, claustrophobic funk, Prince mumbling, then squealing, then slurring about being high, so high. What makes it so hard to dance to is not only its stumbling bassline, in and out of sync with the vocals, but the way those vocals puncture another fantasy. How we don't need reefer, don't need cocaine, how its music that goes straight to his brain and makes him high – so high. 'Purple Music' was recorded in 1982 but only released in 2019 after Prince had died, overdosing on the opiate fentanyl.

Drugs run through dance music like salt through sweat. The structure of the music, whatever its genre, is built around addiction, returning obsessively to the same thing over and over again, discovering that you can never return, that the accumulation of a habit makes a difference. The length of songs, of nights, of days; it pushes you to go further, pulling you back in with its promise of escape.

The history of dance music, especially in the early years I came to treasure, is punctured with death, a different high on every grave. Larry Levan ended up selling all his records to feed a drug habit and died, homeless and ignored, at 38; today, you can read a list documenting every song Levan played at the Paradise Garage online. Ron Hardy, who played alongside Frankie Knuckles in Chicago, helping to define house music, was dead by 1992, forgotten. Maybe the music had nothing to do with these deaths, but maybe there is something cruel in a crowd's relationship to a DJ. Give us our pleasure; spare us your pain.

There is nothing like the absence of drugs to make you feel their presence. The way they can make you abandon your friends after queuing for hours, when by some mystery you get into a club and they don't, since what a night promises seems, for a moment, better than the long work of friendship. How they can make you spend a whole weekend, night and day and night again, in a sprawl of wooden huts beside the Spree in Berlin, at the closing of a club called Bar 25, keeping yourself high for the sole reason of being able to say: I was there. They can leave you staring at a girl having a seizure on a sofa at an after-party in a stranger's house, while hundreds continue that talk, that early morning talk, no longer dancing, no longer listening to the music, no longer able to pretend, amidst all that talk, that it is the music you are addicted to.

12. Röyksopp & Robyn – Monument (Olof Dreijer Remix)

And still, they've always come to pick me up, always let me in in the morning, long after I stopped deserving it. It was never only about the good times, and that is what made all the difference. We discovered we could be brought together by merging in the dark, by touching during a song, by letting go together. And we discovered we could be brought together by going home, by being the right kind of angry, by knowing when to say no.

Friendship leaves few monuments. Love, desire, the passion whose goal is possession: these have founded religions, philosophies and all the poetry I will never read.

Even the songs we sang when we wanted to end the night going back to the start, to those disco anthems, were songs of love: love sensation, love hangover, love is the message. I like to think those songs have lasted and still get played not because love is universal, but that no one ever really listened to them or that when they listened, they heard what they wanted. What was important wasn't the love of the songs we were singing, but that we were singing them together.

With its testimonies so rare, at least in comparison to the libraries of scripts for romantic love, friendship can feel like a journey in the night, like moving with someone through a darkened crowd. It might not even be opposed to love at all; the sex might be better; it might liberate desire from needing to be born from a lack and to seek possession. Or it might be its own whole new sound, a frequency we haven't been trained to hear, our lives still bent to one day growing up, settling down and staying in.

But maybe friendship doesn't need monuments. Maybe its promise lies in its script never being written down, that, unlike romance, there is no plot, no three-minute structure of verse, chorus, consummation. It's a knot that is tied anew each time, between threads already woven with others. And maybe friendships don't need to last; maybe there is care in untying as well as binding. A friendship doesn't have to be for life or be eternal; it can be something woven and loosened in time. Those friends you make for a night: maybe what conjures these friendships into being is the sight not of what you have always been but what you are and want to become. Maybe these friends know more about friendship than anyone. We didn't need a monument to friendship; we went out.

13. *Lone – Hyper Seconds*

Matt Cutler has been making music for just about as long as I have been listening to it. Born and raised in Nottingham, he started in an electro band then made hip-hop before adopting the name of Lone and making dance music that is classical in the sense the term is used in the history of art: working within the rules laid down by a tradition; inheriting, using and extending that tradition. Sometimes this is seen in specific effects like the fades that skitter across 'Hyper Seconds' evoking the futurism of early 1990s raves. Other times, you hear the whole history of dance music replayed across two sides of a record. 'Pineapple Crush / Angel Brain', from 2010, runs back through the stabbing pianos of early house, the robotic pulses and warped synths of Detroit techno, the dreamy melodies of Larry Heard's spiritual house music, right back to a sample of James Brown, the soul music where it all began. Like so much dance music, even as it is now made all over the world, it replays with professed love the history that made it possible, that made our night possible, that made us possible, that made me possible.

A few months after we danced, in June 2020, Theo Parrish, a DJ who grew up in Chicago and lives in Detroit, posted a mixtape online called *We Are Gorgeous Monsterss*. After a couple of weeks, it was taken down and disappeared. The mixtape was a collage weaving together, among other things, speeches about being Black in the United States by James Baldwin and Dave Chapelle, a monologue by a rapper about how electronic music draws from Black people only to forget them and autobiographical reflections from Parrish about being stopped by the police while driving or being kicked off the decks at Berghain, Berlin, for playing hip-hop and soul.

Berghain is for many – not least itself – an icon of global dance music, a club whose allure is based on the same refusal that humiliated Parrish in front of a carefully chosen crowd. Its door policy is notoriously selective; you belong because others do not. One reason is the club's origins in Snax, a gay sex night; the club today retains its conception as a space for gay men to have uninhibited sex, and so, the tourists, sexual and otherwise, must be kept at bay.

Who gets to decide who is a tourist and who is a native? In 2017, the Chicago-born Felix Da Housecat, who started DJing in the early 1990s and who, like many American DJs, released his first records in Europe, becoming more famous there than in his home country if not his home city, was refused entry to Berghain. In his refusal, he posted online, Berghain 'pissed on Frankie Knuckles and Larry Levan', that 'CHIGACO AND DETROIT BUILT BERLIN! TECHNO AND HOUSE', and that 'its not about racist and judging its bout LOVE and a movement'. 'I need 2 figure out a way 2 Make everyone equal, who just wants 2 go to a part and hear good music . . . we are all the same!' 'IM in tears honestly . . .'

Who gets to decide who belongs in a crowd? The decisions are already made. Is remembering their history enough to undo them?

14. Robyn – Got Her Own Thing From Sweden (Kindness Remix)

Happiness is often presented as a feeling, an experience, a private state of being – our own thing. Even when shared, it is the recognition we are all individually feeling the same thing. I feel happy, you feel happy, we feel happy. What we feel is defined as much by what is absent as what is present: no pain, no suffering, no fear, no unease. That absence is what we want to remain present. Happiness aspires to be a state out of time, out of history – forgetting. If that is what happiness is, I should have been able to find it alone in my room. We all should have been able to be happy dancing on our own.

And yet there we were, doing something else, unable to be alone, unable to be together. Separated by our screens, dancing through those screens, we could neither be individuals nor a collective, neither single nor whole. We were a little crowd, a group that is formed, yet whose members remain inaccessible, in the dark, never fully merged into one.

Unable to fulfil the desire to be with one another, we discovered the knowledge of others' concern was enough. Not just the knowledge that you are of concern to others, but that the knowledge that being together, and sustaining being together, is our shared concern. And so that happiness can never be our own thing – something we can control alone. It is the outcome of how we decide to live our lives together.

And that this must take time, not escape it. That it must happen in time, remembering the past, exposed to an unknown future. Happening in a time we can't control; that is the happening in happiness.

15. *Curtis Mayfield – Move On Up*

A snare drum kicks, a trumpet blares: your night is coming to an end. On-screen, Robyn was gesticulating at her decks, pulling out cables. Something had gone wrong, though it seemed like she was fine and happy to give up. Luke and Hannah had gone but had left their phone behind, showing a dark room. Tom was fussing around, tidying up. The girls were dancing together, lost in each other as they always were at the end of a night. I pulled in a chair in front of my desk, wiped the sweat from my screen and sat down with my last cup of wine.

Nights form around their end like songs circle around silence. They are the scaffolding that gives it shape, not an absence that follows a presence. Silence is present around sound, defining its edges, as well as its final destination. So, too, the knowledge a night will end is there from its very beginning; it is the limit that makes all of it possible. That end, that limit – going out is a lesson in finitude.

Sometimes that end disappears as you push on and on; sometimes you know exactly when it will come. Sometimes that decision is made for you in the breakdown of 'Move On Up', a long exhalation, a slow raising of the lights, a reminder to get your coat and go home. Home is where we already were and couldn't help but be.

Sitting in my chair, I was back home, annoyed at the music coming from the kitchen as my Dad cleaned up like he did every weekend, playing the same songs over and over again. American soul: The Temptations, Al Green, Wilson Pickett, Otis Redding. He didn't have many records, just one big Motown compilation and an album of Irish soul covers that he only played, for years, while driving. So much had come from those records, and we had never danced to them.

16. Jamie XX – I Don't Know

Why did we go out?

We went out to dance, drink and disappear.

We went out for the crowd, to be held in movement by strangers.

We went out for the music, though not as often as we liked to think. For Daniel Wang, Girls Aloud, Chaka Khan, BBZ, Larry Heard, Masters at Work, Prins Thomas, Cher, Metro Area, Sippin' Tea, Jayda G, Jodie Harsh, Panti, Midland, Derrick Carter, Lakuti and Tama Sumo.

We went out to gather a litany.

We went out for no reason at all, no reason that we knew.

We went out to come out.

To be someone else: Thalia, Queenie B, Greedy Pig or just a king in a tux.

To wear shoulder pads, culottes, a zebra print hood, leather, fox fur hats, Birkenstock sandals, a harness, sequin, and blood.

To have our bodies moved by someone else's sound.

To be shaped into someone else's form.

We went out to fuck: in clubs, queues, toilets and stairways; beaches, swimming pools, oceans and cinemas; tents, mine and yours.

But also, sometimes just to kiss: a forehead, an arm, a pierced lip, white cotton briefs.

We went out to make mistakes, knowingly and not. To take up too much space, to be 'that bitch', to be ignorant, to hurt people, to make someone feel they wanted to leave, to make each other feel it was time to go home.

We went out to forget.

We went out to be forgotten.

We went out to spend years ending up spending the night talking to Simon, in a park in Berlin, a beach in Croatia, all the houses in Dublin; to be told he thinks you are special, that you need to get out in the world, and to meet him ten years later and be asked: 'How's it going: what's your name?'

We went out because we never did have the perfect night. There was always something: arriving too late, shit sound, a fight at the end, staying out just that little bit too long, the way she was actually being difficult the whole night long but no one said anything to ruin it because, you know what, it was her night.

We went out to give each other what we needed.

We went out to hear the words of the last song:

Happy
Must be happy

Dance with me
Dancing in my head.

I don't know.

WORKS DISCUSSED

Richard Allen, *Skinhead* (London: New English Library, 1970)

Jeremy Atherton Lin, *Gay Bar* (London: Granta Books, 2021)

Alison Bechdel, *Fun Home: A Family Tragicomic* (New York: First Mariner Books, 2006)

Mary E. Bradley Lane, *Mizora* (New York: G. W. Dillingham, 1890)

Wendy Brown, 'Wounded Attachments', *Political Theory* (August, 1993), pp. 390-401

William S. Burroughs, *The Wild Boys: A Book of the Dead* (New York: Grove Press, 1971)

Octavia E. Butler, *Lilith's Brood* (New York: Grand Central, 1989)

Hamad Butt, *Familiars* (Southampton: John Hansard Gallery, 1996)

Lee Edelman, *No Future* (Durham: Duke University Press, 2004)

Shulamith Firestone, *The Dialectic of Sex* (New York: William Morrow, 1970)

Patrick Flanery, *The Ginger Child* (London: Atlantic Books, 2019)

E.M. Forster, *Maurice* (London: Edward Arnold, 1971)

Michel Foucault, *The History of Sexuality* (London: Allen Lane, 1979)

Roxane Gay, *Difficult Women* (London: Corsair, 2017)

Jean Genet, *Our Lady of the Flowers*, trans. Bernard Frechtman, (Paris: Olympia Press, 1957)

Querelle de Brest, trans. Gregory Streatham, (London: Blond, 1966)

Charlotte Gilmore Perkins, *Herland* (New York: Pantheon Book, 1979)

Félix González-Torres, *Untitled (Fortune Cookie Corner)* (1990)

Untitled (Placebo) (1991)

Garth Greenwell, *What Belongs to You* (New York: Farrar, Straus, and Giroux, 2016)

Radclyffe Hall, *The Well of Loneliness* (Paris: Pegasus Press, 1928)

David M. Halperin, *How To Be Gay* (Cambridge, MA: Harvard University Press, 2014)

Saidiya Hartman, 'Interview', *The White Review* 26 (2019)

Uzodinma Iweala, *Speak No Evil* (New York: Harper, 2018)

Derek Jarman, *Dancing Ledge* (London: Quartet, 1984)
Modern Nature: The Journals of Derek Jarman (London: Century, 1991)
At Your Own Risk: A Saint's Testament (London: Hutchinson, 1992).
Smiling in Slow Motion (London: Century, 2000)
Sebastiane (1976)
Jubilee (1978)
The Tempest (1979)
Caravaggio (1986)
The Last of England (1987)
War Requiem (1989)
The Garden (1990),
Edward II (1991)
Wittgenstein (1993)
Blue (1993)

Tomasz Jedrowski, *Swimming in the Dark* (London: Bloomsbury, 2020)

Imre Kertész, *Kaddish for an Unborn Child*, trans. Tim Wilkinson (London: Vintage, 2010)

Olivia Laing, *The Lonely City* (Edinburgh: Canongate, 2016)

Andrea Lawlor, *Paul Takes the Form of a Mortal Girl* (London: Picador, 2017)

Édouard Louis, *The End of Eddy*, trans. Michael Lucey (London: Harvill Secker, 2014)

A History of Violence, trans. Lorin Stein, (London: Harvill Secker, 2018)

Sophie Lewis, *Full Surrogacy Now* (London: Verso, 2019)

Carmen Maria Machado, *In the Dream House* (Minneapolis: Graywolf Press, 2019)

Lois McMaster Bujold, *Ethan of Athos* (Wake Forest: Baen Books, 1986).

Jeremy Mulderig, *The Lost Autobiography of Samuel Steward* (Chicago: Chicago University Press, 2018)

José Esteban Muñoz, *Cruising Utopia* (New York: NYU Press, 2009)

Maggie Nelson, *The Argonauts* (Minnesota: Graywolf Press, 2015)

Catherine Opie, *Self-Portrait (Cutting)* (1993
Justin Bond (1993)
Mike and Sky (1993)
Self-Portrait (Pervert) (1994)
Self-Portrait (Nursing) (2004)

Marge Piercy, *Woman on the Edge of Time* (New York: Knopf, 1976)

Sally Rooney, *Conversation with Friends* (London: Faber, 2017)

Joanna Russ, *The Female Man* (London: Women's Press, 1975)

Joan Slonczewski, *A Door into the Ocean* (London: Women's Press, 1986)

Danez Smith, *[insert] boy* (Portland: Yesyes Books, 2014)
        Homie (London: Vintage, 2020)

Justin Spring, *Secret Historian: The Life and Times of Samuel Steward* (New York: Farrar, Straus, and Giroux, 2010)

Gertrude Stein, *Everybody's Autobiography* (New York: Random House, 1937)

Samuel M. Steward, *Chapters from an Autobiography* (San Francisco: Grey Fox Press, 1981)

Lou Sullivan, *We Both Laughed Along In Pleasure: The Selected Diaries of Lou Sullivan* (New York: Nightboat Books, 2019)

Michelle Tea, *Against Memoir* (New York: Feminist Press, 2018)

Wolfgang Tillmans, *Wolfgang Tillmans* (Köln: Taschen, 1995)
Burg (London: Taschen, 1998)
Soldiers: The Nineties (Köln: Walther König, 1999)
truth study centre (London: Taschen, 2005)
What's Wrong with Redistribution? (London: Taschen, 2015)

Justin Torres, *We the Animals* (London: Granta, 2012)

Michael Warner, ed. *Fear of a Queer Planet* (Minnesota: University of Minnesota Press, 1993)

Jeanette Winterson, *Why Be Happy When You Can Be Normal* (London: Vintage, 2011)

Ocean Vuong, *On Earth We're Briefly Gorgeous* (London: Jonathan Cape, 2019)

Hanya Yanagihara, *A Little Life* (London: Vintage, 2015)

ABOUT THE AUTHOR

Kevin Brazil is a writer and critic who currently lives in Berlin. He grew up in County Wexford, Ireland, and studied English at Trinity College, Dublin, and Oxford. His essays and criticism have appeared in *Granta*, *Frieze*, *The White Review*, the *London Review of Books*, the *Times Literary Supplement*, *Art Review*, *art-agenda*, *Studio International*, and elsewhere.

ACKNOWLEDGEMENTS

Thank you to my indominable agent, Harriet Moore, who lives her vision of Lydia Davis's vision of Roland Barthes' vision of the book as a collaborative enterprise. Thank you to Kit Caless, for seeing it was about memory all along and for helping me reach those I want to reach. Thank you to the editors who saw some of these essays into print: Francesca Wade, Tom Crewe, and Rosanna McLaughlin. To Natasha Onwuemezi for scrupulous editing. Thanks to Ajamu for the walks. To Matthew, for encouraging me to think about Wolfgang and to share myself with the world. To the Bratty Subs: Iggy, June, Marlo, Frey. Thank you, above all, to all my friends: Tom, Oonagh, Sarah, Duffy, Arthur, Jack, Josie, Bella, Luke, Nick, Zara, Sam, Asha: this is for you, with gratitude and love.